# A Manual of

Carter E. Bearden and Jerry F. Potter

HOME MISSION BOARD
Southern Baptist Convention
Atlanta, Georgia

# PROLOGUE

There has been a great need for a manual of the language of signs in a religious setting. This book is provided to meet such a need and may be the forerunner of a comprehensive dictionary of religious signs. Like all living languages, some of the new signs given in the book may be refined in the process and/or changed to meet the pressing needs of the religious communities until they are widely accepted by all denominations.

Mrs. Louis A. Beard, of Houston, Texas, and Jack Hensley, of Austin, Texas, were very helpful with the preparation of religious signs. The author thanks them for their part in the early development of this work.

Jerry Potter, of Thomasville, North Carolina, prepared all the illustrations in this manual and is the coauthor.

The chaplains of Gallaudet College, Washington, D.C., have contributed to the growth of religious signs and have offered invaluable suggestions. They have attempted to standardize the signs in the hope that the deaf and their religious workers may use them in conferences, camps and services.

Special thanks go to Rev. Otto Berg (Episcopal), Rev. Clifford Bruffey (Baptist), Rev. Daniel Pokorny (Lutheran), and Rev. Rudolph Gawlik (Catholic) for their assistance in making this dictionary possible. The author also wishes to thank Mrs. Celia Warshawsky for her contribution to the work on Jewish signs. He acknowledges his indebtedness to Francis Higgins, chairman of the Department of Chemistry at Gallaudet College and minister to the deaf at Calvary Baptist Church, Washington, D.C., for his monumental work in this field; and expresses his deepest gratitude for the many hours Higgins spent on the texts and drawings of religious signs. The final responsibility of the book, however, rests with the author.

It is hoped that this manual will find a wider acceptance among all persons of different faiths, although one will find the sign for "baptism" particular to the Baptist faith and to other denominations that practice immersion. The author is working with leaders of other denominations in the production of new signs to be incorporated in another book that will contain baptism by sprinkling, sacraments and so forth. He welcomes any comment from the reader.

CARTER E. BEARDEN, SR.  *Field Consultant*
Department of Language Missions
Baptist Home Mission Board, SBC

# CONTENTS

Page

Prologue . . . . . . . . . . . . . . . . . . . . . . . . . . . . . . . . . . . . . . . . . ii

Contents . . . . . . . . . . . . . . . . . . . . . . . . . . . . . . . . . . . . . . . . iii

Introduction to the Religious Signs. . . . . . . . . . . . . . . . . . . iv

Explanation of Directions Used . . . . . . . . . . . . . . . . . . . . . vii

Words and Signs. . . . . . . . . . . . . . . . . . . . . . . . . . . . . . . . . . 1

Index . . . . . . . . . . . . . . . . . . . . . . . . . . . . . . . . . . . . . . . . . 189

# INTRODUCTION TO THE RELIGIOUS SIGNS

It is of paramount importance that a learner, who is not familiar with the language of signs, acquaint himself with the suffixes which are given on the next few pages. Once he masters them, he will encounter little difficulty throughout the book. It is also suggested that he read the text in his attempt to learn each new sign. Since greater emphasis is placed on the grace and clarity of the sign movement, it is imperative that a signer (one who signs) form a habit of spelling the letters and/or signing clearly at all times.

## -ER

Place the right flat hand, the fingers pointing forward and the palm facing left, at the right side of the body at chest level. Do the same with the left hand at the left side. Move both hands downward. This sign is to be used to indicate a person such as a teacher, a preacher, a disciple, a saint, and so on.

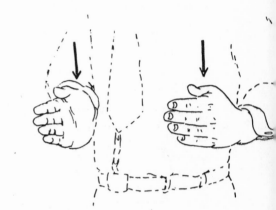

## -MENT

Position the left flat hand in front of self, palm facing right front diagonal. Touch the finger area of the left hand with the right "M" hand, palm facing left front diagonal. Move the right hand down vertically.

## -ION

Position the left flat hand in front of self, palm facing right front diagonal. Touch the finger area of the left hand with the right "I" hand, palm facing left front diagonal. Move the right hand down vertically.

## -NESS

Position the left flat hand in front of self, palm facing right front diagonal. Touch the finger area of the left hand with the right "N" hand, palm facing left front diagonal. Move the right hand down vertically.

## -EOUS

Position the left flat hand in front of self, palm facing right front diagonal. Touch the finger area of the left hand with the right "O" hand, palm facing left front diagonal. Move the right hand down vertically.

## -TION

Position the left flat hand in front of self, palm facing right front diagonal. Touch the finger area of the left hand with the right "T" hand, palm facing left from diagonal and the "T" touching. Move the right hand down vertically.

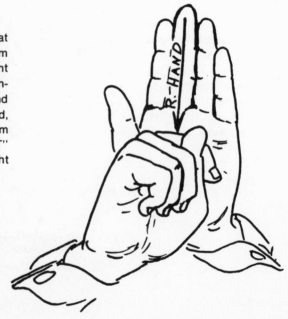

# EXPLANATION OF DIRECTIONS USED

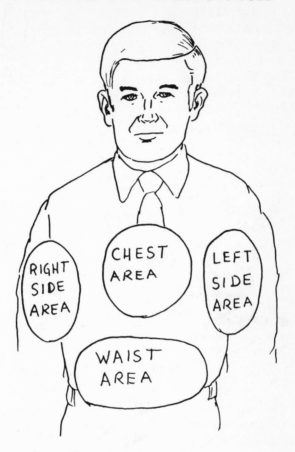

Figure 1

Figure 1 depicts the area
where the hands are to be
positioned.

Figure 2

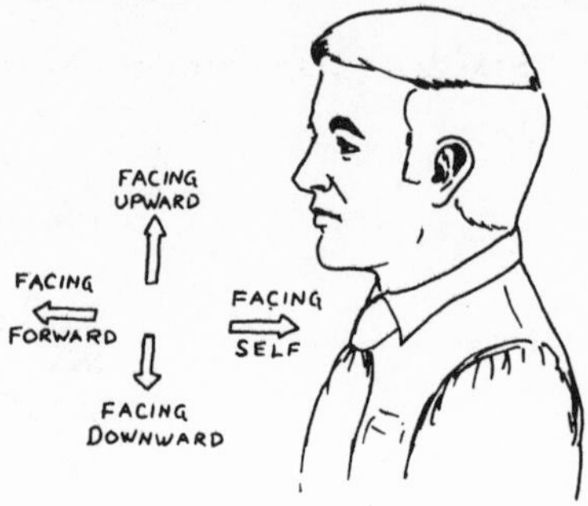

FACING
UPWARD

FACING
FORWARD

FACING
SELF

FACING
DOWNWARD

Figure 3

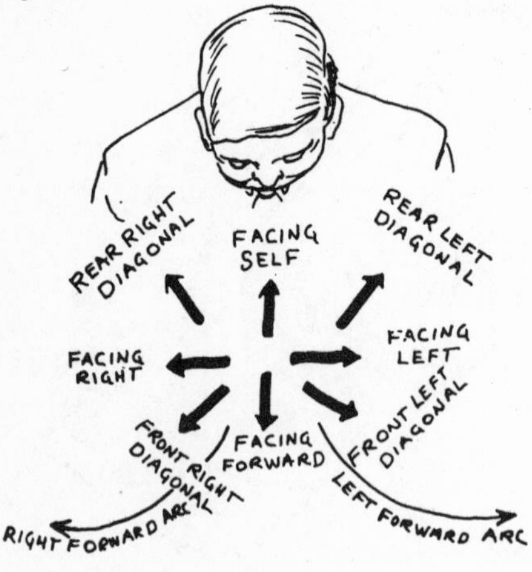

REAR RIGHT
DIAGONAL

FACING
SELF

REAR LEFT
DIAGONAL

FACING
RIGHT

FACING
LEFT

FRONT RIGHT
DIAGONAL

FACING
FORWARD

FRONT LEFT
DIAGONAL

RIGHT FORWARD ARC

LEFT FORWARD ARC

Figures 2 and 3 show the
positions of the palms as
well as the directions in
which the hands move.

Figure 4

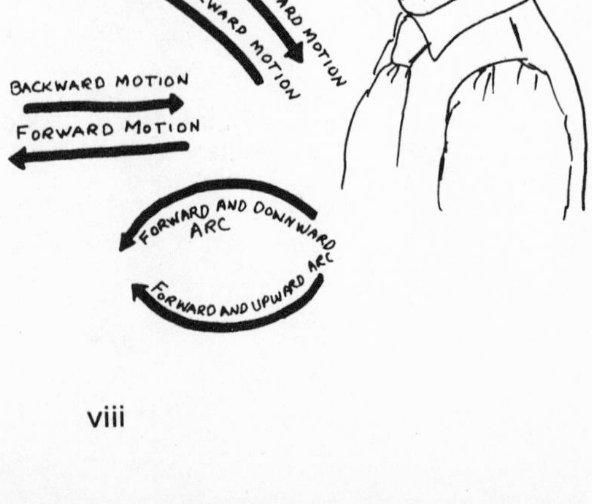

REARWARD AND DOWNWARD MOTION

UPWARD AND FORWARD MOTION

BACKWARD MOTION

FORWARD MOTION

FORWARD AND DOWNWARD
ARC

FORWARD AND UPWARD ARC

Figure 4 shows the direc-
tions in which the hands
are to move.

viii

## ADULTERY

Sexual unfaithfulness of a husband or wife.

Place the left "V" hand, the palm facing self, in front of you. Touch the left index finger with the right "A" hand, the palm facing left. Then touch the left middle finger with the right hand, still in the "A" position.

1

## ALTAR

Table or stand in the most sacred part of a church, synagogue or temple; any high place on which sacrifices are offered.

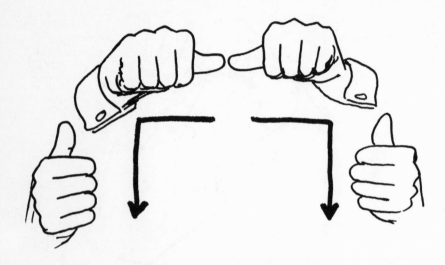

With the hands in the "A" position, both palms facing down, bring to touch the thumbs of both hands in front of self. Now move both hands horizonally away from each other. Then bring both "A" hands down, the palms facing each other.

# ANGEL

Messenger of God.

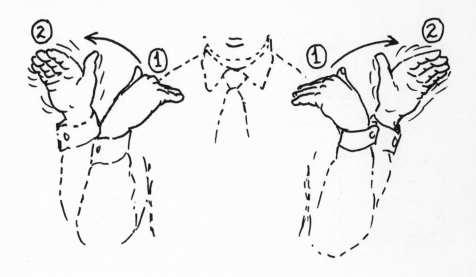

Put the fingertips of both hands to the shoulders and then spread the arms outward, about a foot apart from the shoulders. With the arms in the outward position, wave the hands, palms facing forward, back and forth at least twice. This conveys the idea of a person with a pair of wings.

# ANOINT

Put oil on; consecrate by applying oil.

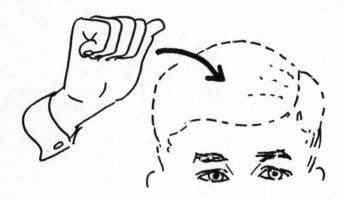

Place the right "A" hand over the head. Now turn the hand downward to the left as if pouring oil on the head.

## APOSTASY (APOSTATE)

Complete forsaking of one's religion.

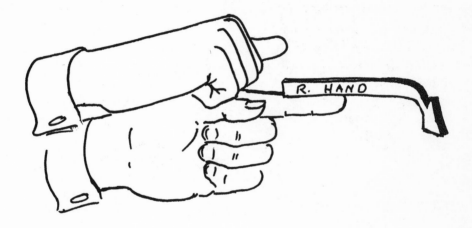

Place the right "A" hand, palm facing down, on top of the left closed hand, its index finger pointing forward and its palm facing right. Move the right "A" hand slightly forward and then to the right in a quarter arc. (Add "er" for "apostate.")

# APOSTLE

One of the twelve disciples of Christ; Christian leader or missionary; leader of any reform or belief.

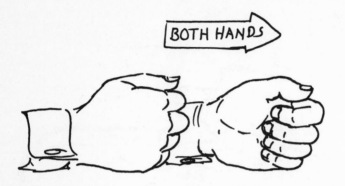

Place the right "A" hand about three or four inches behind the left "A" hand in a front left diagonal direction from each other. Move both hands forward in a manner similar to the sign for "follow," ending with the sign for "-er."

# ATONE (MENT)

Reconciliation of God with sinners through the death of Christ.

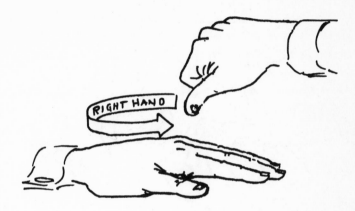

RIGHT HAND

Place the left flat hand, the palm facing downward, in front of self. Now move the right "A" hand, palm facing downward, over the back of the left hand in a counterclockwise motion. This conveys the idea of blood "pouring over" the altar. For "atonement," add the sign for "-ment."

# ATTITUDE

Manner toward a person or thing.

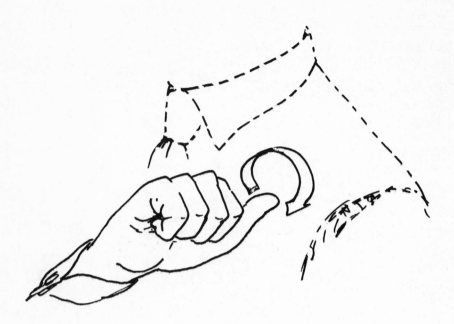

Move the right "A" hand, palm facing left, in a clockwise motion over the heart or the left chest, ending with a touch on the chest.

# AUTHORITY

Legal power to enforce obedience; influence that creates respect; source of correct information.

Touch the left shoulder with the right "A" hand, palm facing downward. Bring the right "A" hand down to rest on the lower portion of the bent left arm, the palm of the right hand facing the upper portion of the bent arm. This is similar to the sign for "power."

## BACKSLIDE (R)

Slide back into wrongdoing.

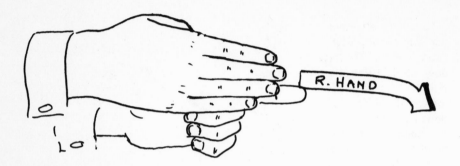

Touch the outer edge of the left index finger pointing forward, its palm facing right, with the middle finger of the right "B" hand, the palm facing left. Now move the right "B" hand slightly forward in the right forward arc. Add the sign "-er" for "backslider."

# BAPTIST

Member of a Christian church that believes in baptism by dipping the whole person under water.

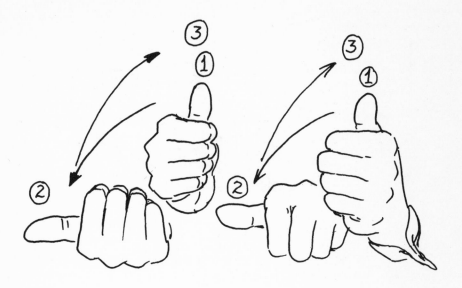

With the hands in a parallel horizonal "A" position, the thumbs pointing upward and the palms facing each other, move both hands in a quarter downward arc to the right and then back to their original position. Add the sign "-er" whenever a person of the Baptist faith is mentioned.

11

## BAPTIZE (ISM)

Dip into water.

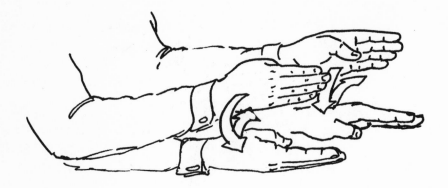

With the hands in a parallel "B" position, the palms facing each other, move both hands in a motion similar to the sign for "Baptist." This sign is used whenever speaking of water baptism or immersion.

# BELIEVE (BELIEF)

Accept as true or real; have faith in; trust.

Touch the forehead with the right index finger and bring the right hand down to clasp the left hand, both palms facing each other.

# BEATITUDES

Supreme happiness; bliss; Bible verses beginning "Blessed are the poor in spirit."

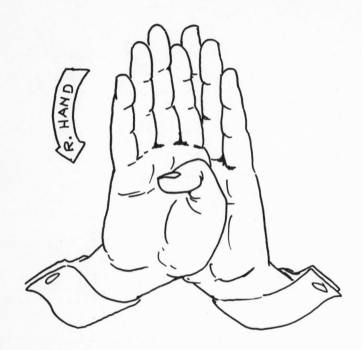

Place the left hand, the palm being open flat and facing front right diagonal, in front of self. Touch the upper portion of the left palm with the right "B" hand, its palm facing front left diagonal. In a rapid succession, move the right hand down to touch the lower portion of the left palm. It is the same as the sign for "rule," except for the right "B" stance. This conveys the idea of the Beatitudes as "golden rules" for Christian living.

14

# BIBLE

The collection of sacred writings of the Christian religion.

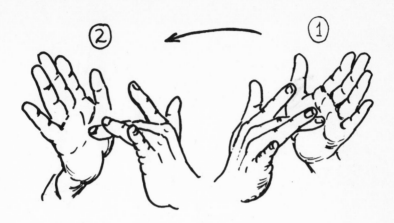

Touch the left open palm with the tip of the right middle finger. Then touch the right open palm with the left middle finger. Bring both hands together, the palms being opened flat and facing each other. Keep the little fingers in contact while moving the hands in the opposite backward direction.

## BIBLE

The collection of sacred writings of the Christian religion.

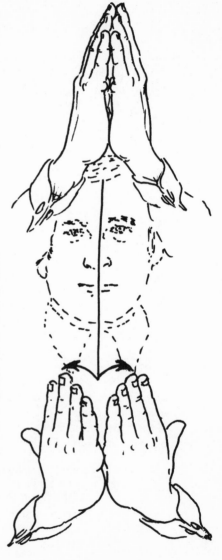

New sign acceptable to Jews and Christians alike in interfaith conferences: Bring both hands together, the palms being opened flat and facing each other. Position the hands above the head level in front of self. Now lower the hands toward self until they are several inches away from the chest. Then open the hands in the opposite backward direction while keeping the little fingers in contact. This sign movement conveys the idea of a book (Word) coming from God.

## BLASPHEMY

Abuse or contempt for God.

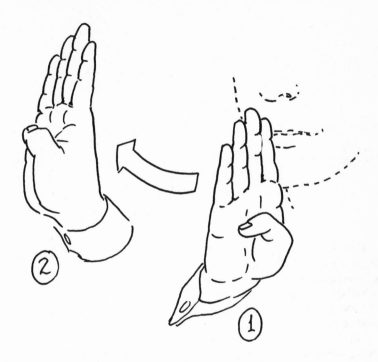

Touch the lips with the right "B" hand, the palm facing left. Now move the hand away from the lips, turning the palm of the right "B" hand to face forward and slightly upward as if in defiance of God.

17

# BLESS (ING)

Ask God's favor for; wish good to; make happy or successful; praise; glorify.

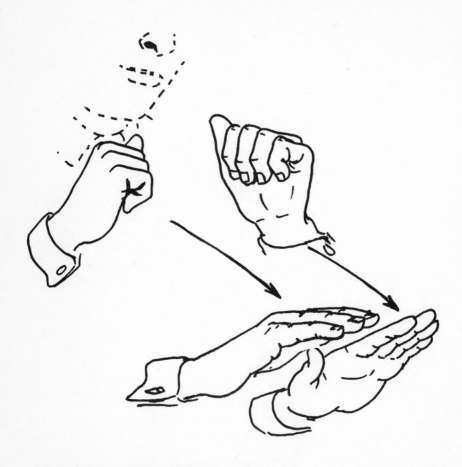

With both hands in the "A" position, the palms facing downward, place the right hand in front of self at chin level and the left hand several inches away and to the left of the right hand. Flip both wrists slightly forward and upward. Open the fingers at the same time when flipping the wrists. Then let both hands fall, palms downward.

# BLOOD

Red liquid in veins and arteries; bloodshed; slaughter.

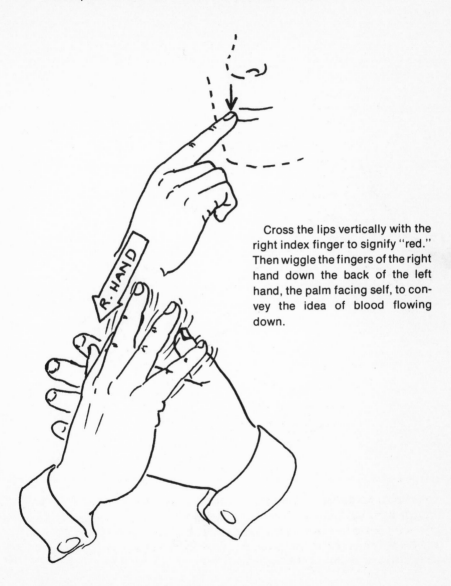

Cross the lips vertically with the right index finger to signify "red." Then wiggle the fingers of the right hand down the back of the left hand, the palm facing self, to convey the idea of blood flowing down.

# BOARD OF DEACONS

A group of deacons. (See "deacon.")

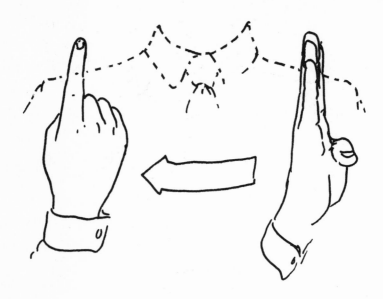

Touch the left shoulder with the right "B" hand, palm facing left, and then the right shoulder with the "D" hand, palm facing self, while changing from "B" to "D" in a rightward motion.

# BURDEN

Load.

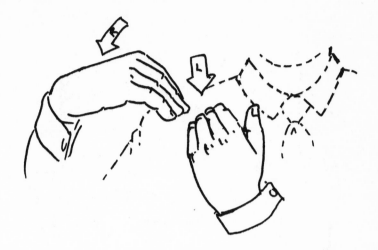

Place the tips of both hands, the palms being opened and facing down, on the right shoulder. Press them once while bringing both bent arms slightly down and closer to the body.

# CELEBRATE (TION)

Observe with the proper ceremonies.

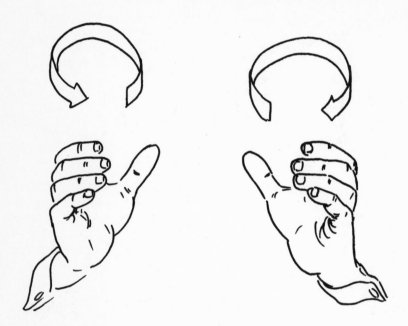

With both hands in the "C" position, palms facing each other, in front of self, move the right hand in a counter-clockwise motion and the left hand in the clockwise motion twice. Add the sign "-tion for "celebration."

22

# CHAPTER

A main division of a book or other writing.

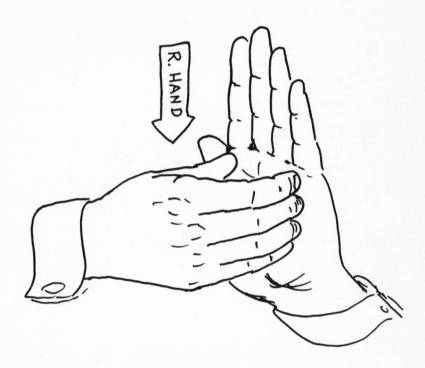

Place the left open hand in front of self, the palm facing front right diagonal and the fingers pointing upward. Brush the outer edges of the left palm with the right "C" hand, palm facing the left palm, in a downward motion.

23

# CHARACTER

Nature; moral strength or weakness; reputation; special quality that makes one person.

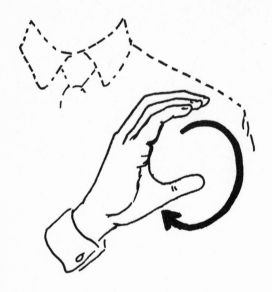

Move the right "C" hand in a clockwise circle over the heart, the palm facing left, with the thumb resting very lightly on the chest at the end of the movement. Add the sign "-er" when referring to a person.

# CHOIR

Group of singers used in a church service.

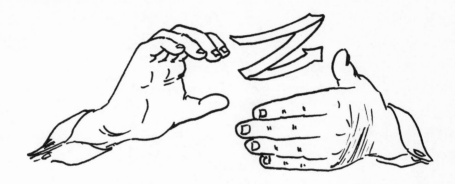

Place the left open hand in midair, the palm facing self. Move the right "C" hand, the palm facing the left palm, left and right across the left hand.

# CHRIST

Jesus the founder of Christian religion; the "Anointed One" of God.

# CHRISTIAN

Believer in Christ (noun); showing a gentle, helpful spirit (adj.); of Christ or his teaching (adj.).

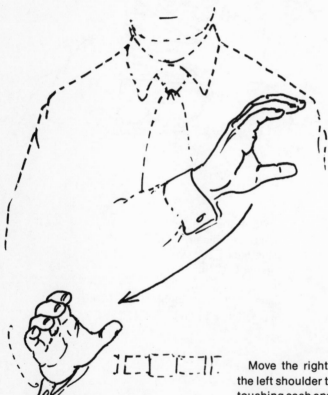

Move the right "C" hand from the left shoulder to the right waist, touching each end with the thumb.

Make the sign for "Christ" and then add the sign for "-er" to denote a person who believes in or follows Christ.

# CHURCH

A building for public Christian worship; religious service in a church; all Christians.

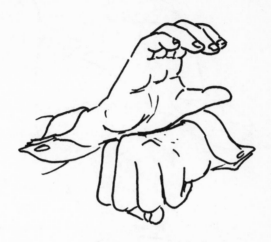

Strike the back of the left "S" hand, the palm facing downward, with the thumb of the right "C" hand, palm facing front left diagonal, lightly. Then let the right hand rest on the back of the left hand.

## CLEANSE

To make clean.

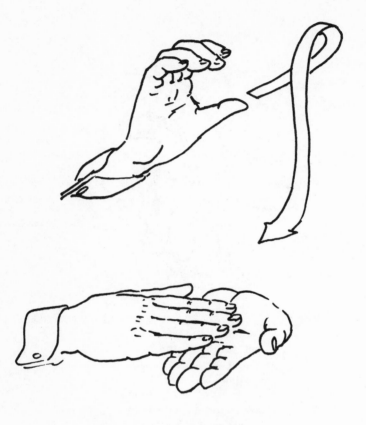

Position the left open upward palm in front of self. Place the right "C" hand, palm facing front left diagonal, above the left hand. Now move the right hand in a (forward, downward and backward) semicircular motion while changing it from a "C" to a flat downward palm. Let the right palm touch the left palm nearest the wrist. Then move the right hand across the left palm, the sign being the same as that for "clean."

28

# CLERGY

Ministers, pastors, and priests.

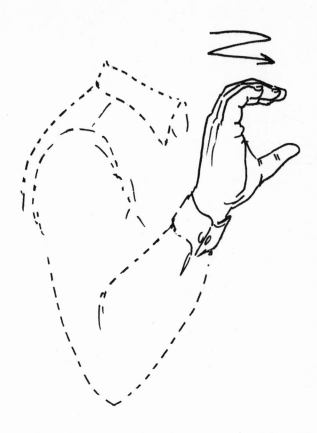

Wave the right "C" hand, palm facing forward, back and forth at least twice, ending the movement with a sign for "-er."

## COMMUNION

Intimate talk; fellowship; group of people having the same religious beliefs; celebration of the Lord's Supper.

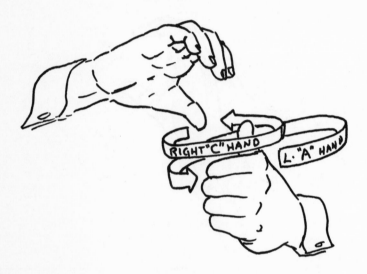

RIGHT "C" HAND    L. "A" HAND

Move the right "C" hand, the palm facing front left diagonal, in a counterclockwise circle over the left thumb of the "A" hand moving in the opposite circle. It is the same as the sign for "fellowship," except that the right hand is in the "C" position.

# CONDEMN (ATION)

Express strong disapproval; pronounce guilty of crime or wrong; declare not sound or suitable for use.

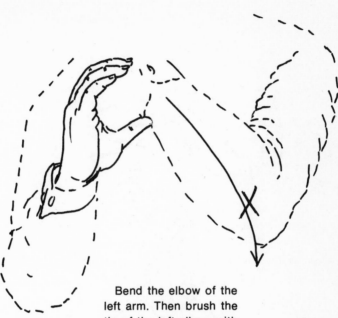

Bend the elbow of the left arm. Then brush the tip of the left elbow with the outer edge of the index finger of the right "C" hand, palm facing left, in a downward stroke. It is the same as the sign for "punishment." Add the sign for "-tion" for "condemnation," except that the right hand is in the "C" stance, to be followed by the sign "-tion" for "condemnation."

31

# CONSCIENCE

A sense of right and wrong.

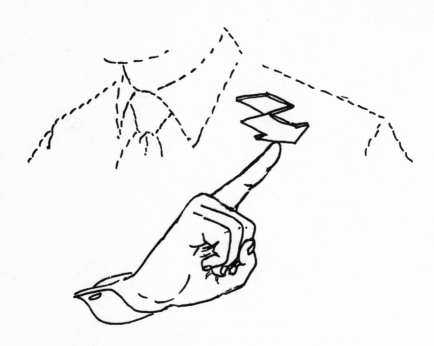

Strike at least twice the left chest
or heart area with the outer edge
of the index finger of the right
hand, palm facing left.

## CONSECRATE (TION)

Set apart as holy or sacred.

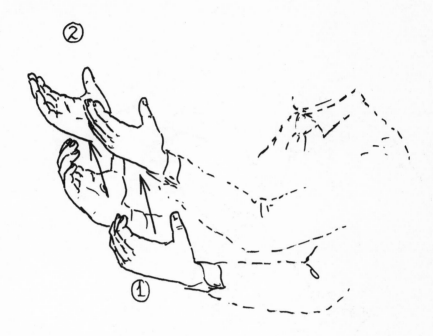

With both hands in the "C" position, palms facing upward, bring both hands up while opening them into flat upward palms as if making a sign for "offer." For "consecration," add the sign "-tion."

# CONVERT (SION)

Turning; changing; act of changing from unbelief to faith.

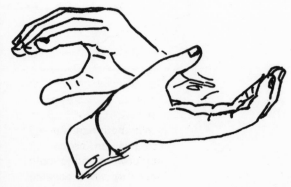

Place the wrist of the right "C" hand on the wrist of the left "C" hand, the right palm facing down at a slant while the left palm is facing up at a slant. Turn the wrists in a clockwise motion, still touching each other, so as to bring the top right hand under and the under left hand to the top. Add the sign "er" to indicate a person (convert). It is the same as the sign for "change," except for the "C" position.

## CONVICT (ION)

Prove guilty; act of declaring guilty; firm belief.

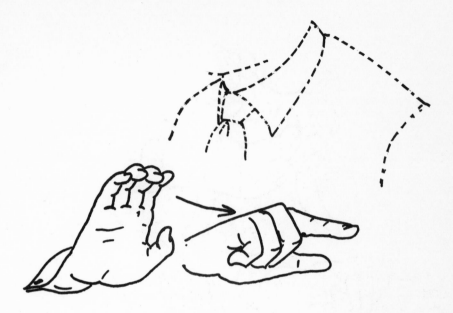

Place the right "C" hand over the heart or left chest. Then change it to a "G" while moving the hand to touch the heart or chest area of the body, the outer edges of the right index finger and thumb of the "G" hand touching the chest several times. This conveys the idea of the person being *guilty* of some sin. For "Conviction," add the sign "-ion."

# CORRUPT (ION)

Wickedness; rot; decay; bribery and dishonesty.

Place both "C" hands in front of self, the palms facing each other. Now close the thumb of each hand to touch the middle finger of the same hand and to rub over the index finger, ending in the "thumbs up" position. It is the same as the sign for "disappear" or "rot away," except that the motion begins with a "C" position.

# COVENANT

A solemn agreement.

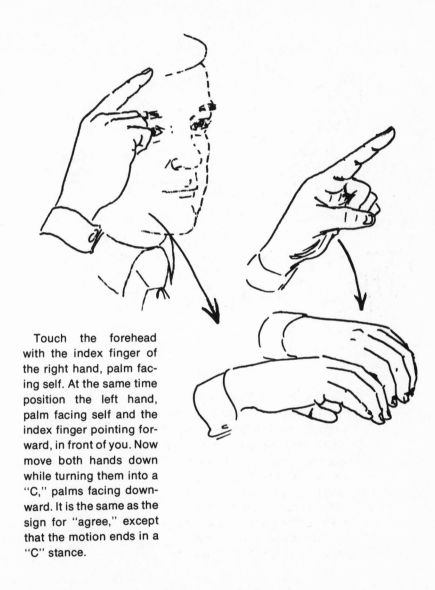

Touch the forehead with the index finger of the right hand, palm facing self. At the same time position the left hand, palm facing self and the index finger pointing forward, in front of you. Now move both hands down while turning them into a "C," palms facing downward. It is the same as the sign for "agree," except that the motion ends in a "C" stance.

# CREED

Brief statement of essential points of religious beliefs; any statement of faith.

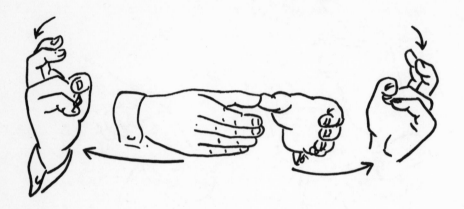

With both hands in the "C" position, the palms facing each other and the thumbs touching each other, wiggle both hands while moving them away from each other in the opposite horizonal direction. It is the same as the sign for "sentence" or "statement," except for the "C" position.

# CROSS

A stick or post with another across it; cross on which Christ died.

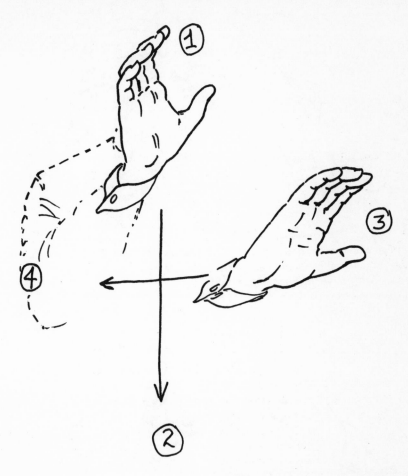

Make the sign of the cross with the right "C" hand, the palm facing forward, beginning with a vertical downward and then a horizonal movement to the right.

# CROWN

(verb) To make king or queen; honor. (noun) A head covering for a king or queen.

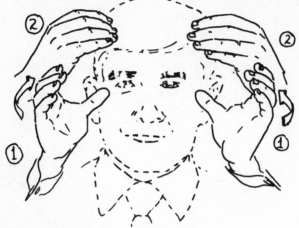

*Noun:* With both hands in the "C" position, the palms facing each other, place them above the head. Move both hands down as if putting a "crown" on the head.

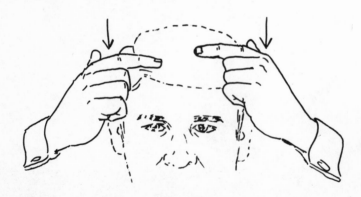

*Verb:* With both hands closed and the index fingers and thumbs extending, position them above the head. Now move both hands down as if "crowning" the head.

## CRUCIFY (IXION)

Put to death by nailing to a cross.

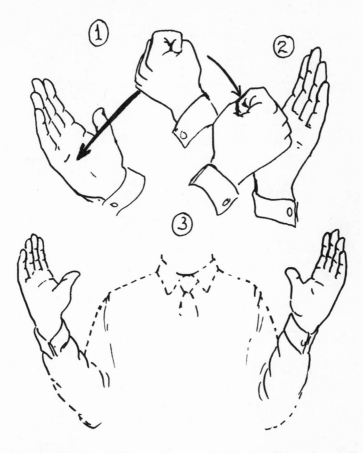

Hit the left flat palm with the right "S" hand, the edge of the small closed finger and palm touching. Then hit the right flat palm with the left "S" hand in the same manner. (This conveys the idea of nails oeing driven into the palms.) In a rapid succession, place both hands in front of self, the right hand slightly beyond your right side and the left hand slightly beyond your left side, both palms facing forward.

41

# DAMN (ATION)

Declare to be bad; condemn; condemn to hell.

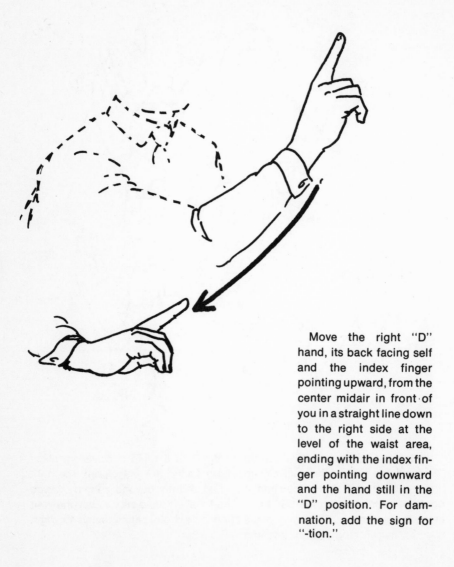

Move the right "D" hand, its back facing self and the index finger pointing upward, from the center midair in front of you in a straight line down to the right side at the level of the waist area, ending with the index finger pointing downward and the hand still in the "D" position. For damnation, add the sign for "-tion."

## DARE

Be bold; have courage; not to be afraid.

Place the left "D" hand in front of self, its palm facing self. Now place the right "D" hand several inches nearer the chest, its palm facing the left palm. Move both hands diagonally to the left. It is the same as the sign for "challenge," except in the "D" position.

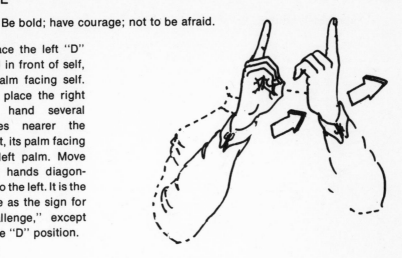

## DEACON

Officer of a church who helps the minister.

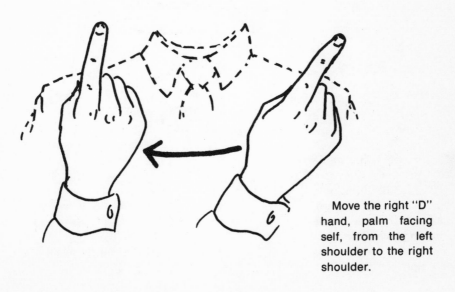

Move the right "D" hand, palm facing self, from the left shoulder to the right shoulder.

## DEDICATE (ION)

Set apart for a purpose.

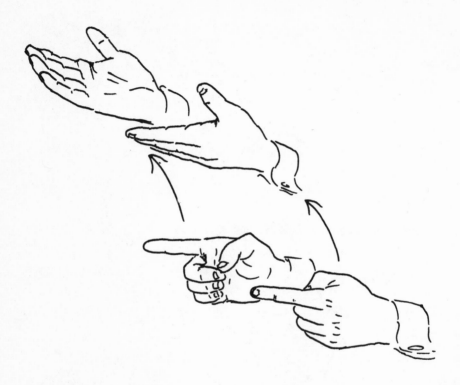

With both hands in the "D" position, palms facing each other, bring both hands in a forward, upward motion while opening them, palms facing upward as if making the sign for "offer."

## DENOMINATION

Religious group or sect.

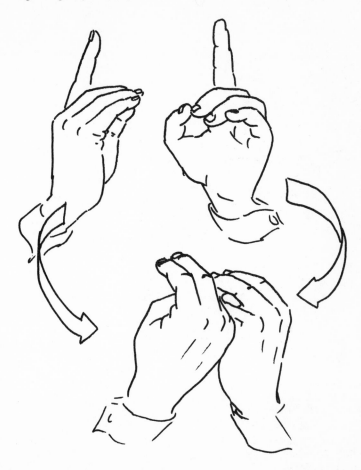

    With both hands in the "D" position, both "D's" touching each other and the back of both hands facing self, bring each hand around in a semicircle away from self. Change the sign from "D" to "N" while the hands are in motion until the sides of the little fingers and palms of the "N" hands touch each other. This denotes the idea of a class, group or body of people of the same inclination.

## DENY (IAL)

Declare (something) is not true; refuse; disown.

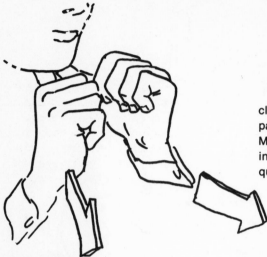

Place the thumbs of both closed hands under the chin, palms facing each other. Move them away from the chin in a slightly downward quarter-arc motion.

## DEPARTMENT

A separate part or division.

With both hands in the "D" position, both "D's" touching each other and the back of both hands facing self, bring each hand around in a semicircle away from self until the sides of the little fingers and palms touch each other. This is the same as the sign for "class," "group," and "family," except that the hands are in the "D" position.

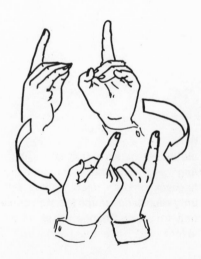

## DESTINY

What becomes of person or thing in the end.

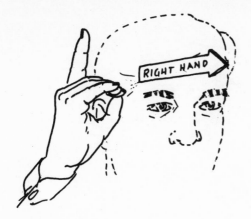

Place the right "D" hand near the right side of the face at eye level. Move it forward, keeping the index finger in a slanted skyward position while in motion. It is the same as the sign for "future," except for the "D" position.

## DEVIL (SATAN)

Satan; wicked or cruel person.

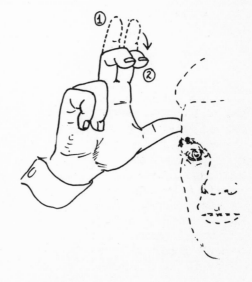

Place the tip of the right thumb at the side of the temple with the index and middle fingers bent and the other two fingers closed. Bend and unbend the index and middle fingers of the right hand at least twice.

47

## DEVOTE (ION)

Give up to some person, purpose, or service; dedicate; consecrate. Deep, steady affection; prayer.

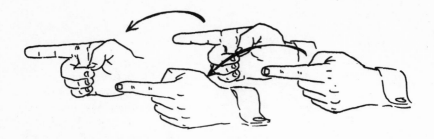

Place the back part of the thumb of the right "D" hand on the chest and the left "D" hand slightly forward and to the left of the right hand. Move both "D" hands in a forward and downward arc. Add the sign for "-tion."

# DISCIPLE

Believer in the thought and teaching of a leader; a follower.

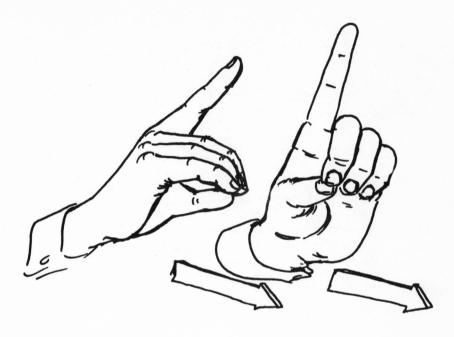

With both hands in the "D" position, place the right hand two or three inches behind the left hand in a left diagonal but horizonal position. Move both hands front left diagonal, ending with the sign for "-er."

TOP VIEW

49

## DISCIPLINE

Training of mind and character; punishment.

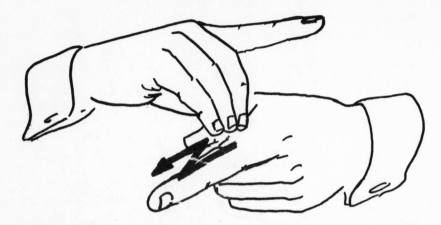

Brush back and forth along the outer side of the left index finger, palm facing right, with the tips of the thumb and middle finger of the right "D" hand. This conveys the idea of *training* of mind and character.

## DIVINE

Of, by, or from God; to or for God; heavenly.

Move the right "D" hand forward, palm facing down, across the left flat, upward hand.

# DOCTRINE

What is taught as the belief of a church; teachings.

Position the left "D" hand near the left side of the face at eye level, the palm facing right. Now position the right "D" hand near the right side of the face, the palm facing left. Move both hands forward, backward, and then forward again. The idea of *teaching,* i.e. doctrine, is intended here.

# DOOM

Ruin; judgment.

Brush forward once the outside upper edge of the left "D" hand, palm facing right, with the lower edge of the right "D" hand, palm facing left, ending with a right downward motion.

R. HAND

# EASTER

Day for celebrating Christ's rising from the dead.

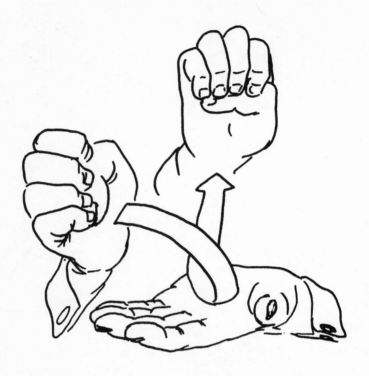

Place the right "E" hand, palm facing left, slightly at the level of and to the right of the left upward, flat palm. Move the right hand to land on the left palm, both palms facing each other. Then lift up the right "E" hand, its back facing self. This conveys the idea of the resurrection.

## EFFECTIVE

Producing desired effect; active; impressive.

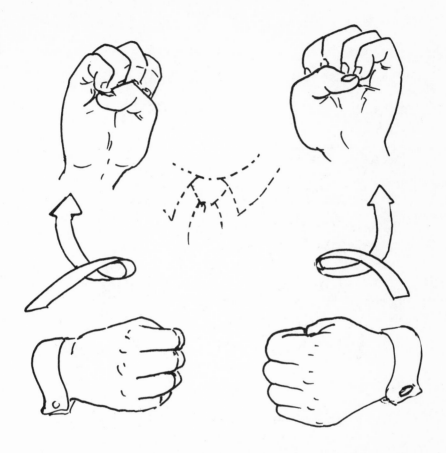

With both hands in the "E" position, the palms facing self, place the right hand to the front right side of self and the left hand to the front left side. Flip the wrists slightly downward and then outward, the left hand moving in a counterclockwise arc and the right hand in a clockwise arc. It is the same as the sign for "success" or "successful," except that the hands are in the "E" position.

# ELECT

Choose.

Place the right "E" hand very close to the index finger of the left "V" hand, both palms facing each other. Move the right "E" hand away from the left hand. It is the same as the sign for "choose," except that the right hand is in the "E" stance.

# EPISTLE

Letter written by one of Christ's apostles to various churches and individuals.

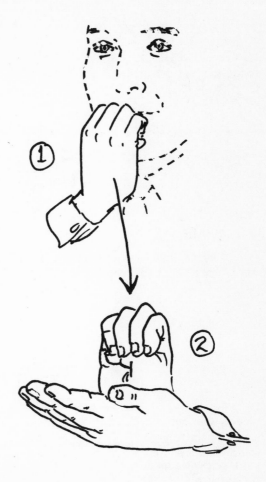

Touch lightly the area of lips and chin with the right "E" hand, palm facing self. Bring the right hand down so as to rest it on the left open flat palm which is positioned in midair at the chest level and facing slantwise toward self. Be sure that the "E," the back of the right hand facing self, is visible beyond the left palm.

## ETERNAL

Without beginning or ending; always and forever the same.

Move the right "E" hand, palm facing forward, first in a clockwise circle and then forward.

## ETHICS (AL)

Of ethics (standards of right and wrong) and morality; in accordance with formal rules of right and wrong.

Place the right "E" hand, the palm facing left, near the heart and move it in a clockwise motion, ending with the back thumb of the "E" hand resting slightly on the heart area.

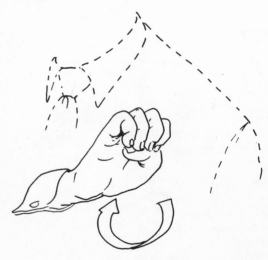

## EVANGELICAL (ISM)

According to the four Gospels of the New Testament; adherent of evangelical doctrine; having to do with Protestant churches that emphasize Christ's atonement and salvation by faith.

## EVANGELIST

Preacher of the Gospel; traveling preacher who stirs up religious feelings in revivals and camp services.

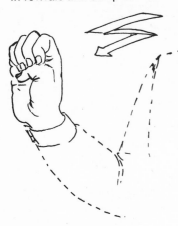

Move the right "E" hand at shoulder height, palm facing forward, forward and backward at least twice. Add "-er" for "evangelist."

## EVERLASTING

Lasting forever; eternity.

Move the right "E" hand, palm facing forward, in a clockwise circle. At the completion of the circle change from "E" to "Y" and then move the "Y" hand forward. It is the same sign as that for "forever," except that the letters "E" and "Y" are used, instead.

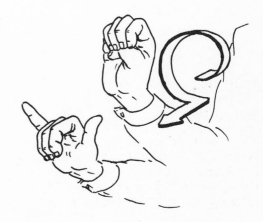

# EXALT (ATION)

Raise in rank, honor, power, et cetera; praise, honor, or glorify.

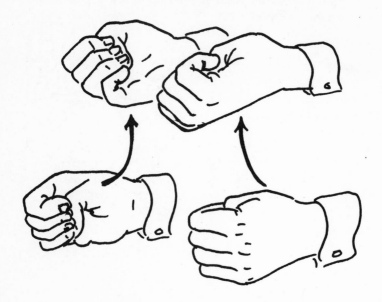

With both hands in the "E" position, palms facing downward, place them in front of you, the right hand to the right and the left hand to the left. At the same time move the hands toward each other in a semicircle, turning the palms upward as you do. The "E" hands will come within several inches of each other, palms facing upward. Continue moving both hands straight up. It is the same as the sign for "lift" or "lift up," but both hands are in the "E" stance.

## EXAMPLE (EMBLEM)

A model, pattern or sample.

Place the right "E" hand, palm facing front left diagonal, on the left open hand, palm facing front right diagonal. Move both hands forward. It is the same as the sign for "show," except that the right hand is in the "E" position.

## EXHORT (ATION)

Urge strongly.

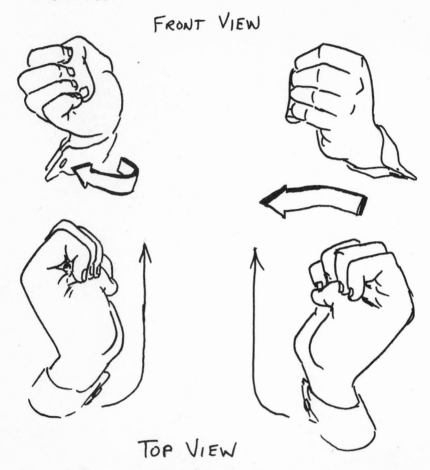

FRONT VIEW

TOP VIEW

With the hands in the "E" position, palms slightly facing each other, place them in front of you, the right hand to the right and the left hand to the left. Move both hands in circles, the left hand in the front right diagonal counterclockwise and the right hand in a front left diagonal clockwise motion. It is the same as the sign for "encourage," except for the "E" position.

# FAITH

A believing without proof; belief in God.

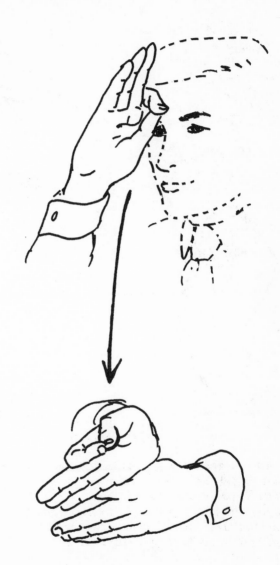

Place the tips of the thumb and index finger of the right "F" hand, palm facing left, on the right side of the forehead lightly. At the same time, position the left "F" hand, palm facing right, in the center midair in front of self. Bring the right "F" hand to rest on top of the left "F" hand.

## FAITHFUL

Loyal; true; (the faithful) the true believers or loyal followers.

Rest the right "F" hand, palm facing left, on top of the left "F" hand, palm facing right. Let the upper right "F" hand jump forward to rest again on top of the lower left "F" hand which moves forward a little to receive the upper hand on top of it.

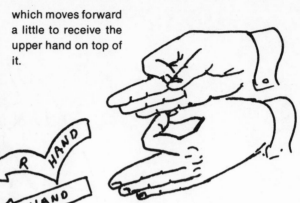

## FAST

Go without food; time or day of fasting.

Position the right "F" hand, palm facing left, at the left end of the lips. Move it across the lips to the right as if sealing the lips.

# FAULT

Mistake; something that is not as it should be.

Place the tips of both "F" hands on the right shoulder and press them once while bringing both bent arms slightly down and closer to the body.

# FAVOR

Kindness; approval, liking; give more than fair treatment to; gift.

With both hands in the "F" position, place the right hand above the left hand, both palms facing toward self. Move both hands in a clockwise circle with the right hand ending at the top. It is the same as the sign for "kindness," except that the hands are in the "F" stance.

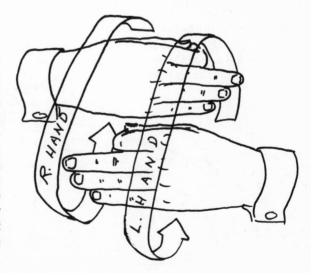

# FIELD

Flat space of land; sphere of activity.

Bring to touch the tips of the thumbs and index fingers of both "F" hands, both palms facing each other, at least one to two feet away from self. Move the right hand in a semicircle away from the left hand which is also moving in a semicircle away from the right hand. At the end of the circle near the chest, have the tips of the thumbs and index fingers of both "F" hands touch again. This sign is to be used when speaking of "area" or "place" as in "mission *field*."

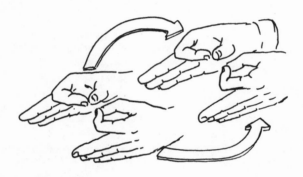

Line of work ("field of work"): Move forward the right "F" hand, palm facing left, across the outer edge of the left "B" hand, palm facing right.

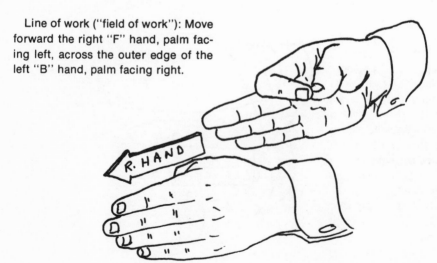

# FLESH

Meat; body; family or relation by birth.

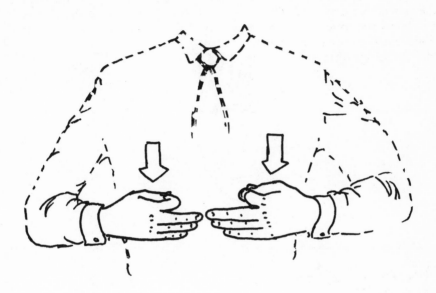

With both hands in the "F" position, palms facing self, place them on the chest (lung area.) Move both hands down in a slight curve to touch the waist. It is the same as the sign for "body," except the hands are in the "F."

# FLOOD

Flow of water over what is usually dry land.

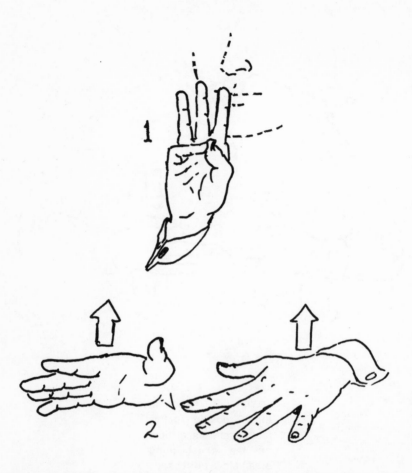

Touch lightly the lower or both lips with the right "W" hand, palm facing left. This is the sign for "water." Then bring it down with the thumb and fingers in a spread fashion, palm downward. At the same time place the left hand in a similar spread fashion. Bring both hands upward to convey the idea of the rising or swelling of water.

# FOLLOW (ER)

Go or come after; go along with.

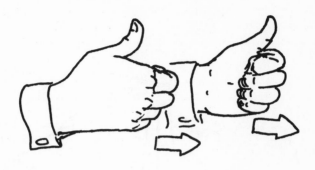

With both hands in the "A" position, the thumbs extending, place the right hands two or three inches behind the left hand in a left front diagonal but horizonal position. Move both hands front left diagonal. When using the term "follower," end the motion with a sign for "-er."

TOP VIEW

# FORETELL

Predict.

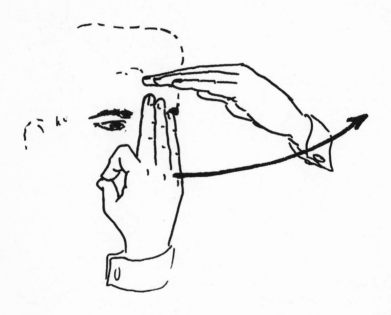

Move the right "F" hand, forward, palm facing self, away from the face and under the left flat downward palm which is positioned in midair and slanted toward self. It is the same as the sign for "prophecy," except that the right hand is in the "F" position.

# FOREVER

Without ever coming to an end; always.

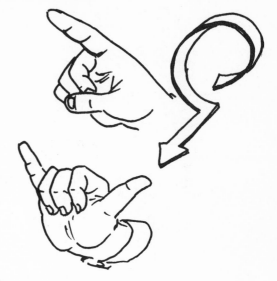

Move the right index finger in a clockwise circle in front of self. At the completion of the circle, change it into a "Y" position and move it forward.

# FORGIVE (NESS)

Give up the wish to punish or get even with; pardon.

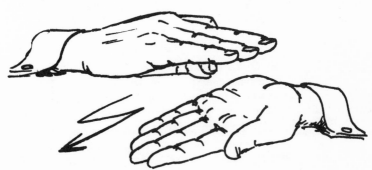

Brush the finger area of the left upward palm with the finger area of the right "F" hand, palm facing downward, at least twice, moving forward each time. Add the sign for "-ness."

69

# FREEWILL

Of one's own accord; freedom of decision.

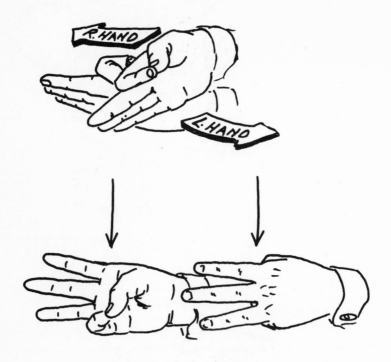

Place the wrist of the right "F" hand, palm facing left, on top of the wrist of the left "F" hand, palm facing right. Move both hands away from each other in a horizonal direction. Then change rapidly from "F" to "W" and bring both "W" hands straight down. Actually, this is two signs in one continuous movement: "free" to "decide."

# FRUIT

Product; result.

Place the right "F" hand, the outer edge of the thumb and index finger touching, against the left flat palm, the fingers of both hands (except right index finger) pointing skyward. Move both hands forward. It is the same as the sign for "show," except the right hand is in the "F" position to convey the idea of the result, example, or fruit of the Spirit.

# FUNERAL

Ceremonies performed when a dead person's body is buried or burned.

With the hands in the "V" position, palms facing forward and the fingertips of the "V's" pointing upward, place the right hand several inches behind the left hand in a diagonal stance. Move both hands front left diagonal.

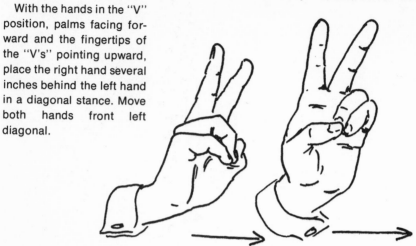

# GLORY (IFY)

Give glory to; priase; worship.

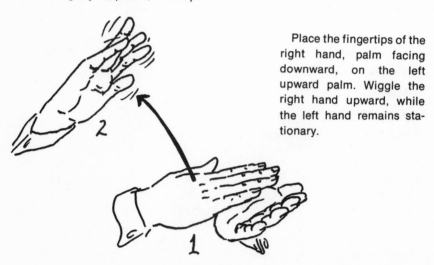

Place the fingertips of the right hand, palm facing downward, on the left upward palm. Wiggle the right hand upward, while the left hand remains stationary.

# GOD

Maker and ruler of the world.

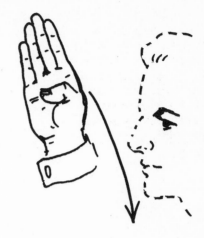

Point upward with the right "B" hand, palm facing left, in front of self. Draw it in a rearward and downward motion, the fingertips still facing skyward.

## GODLY

Pious; devout (religious).

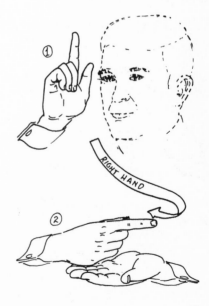

Point upwardly the right "G" hand, palm facing left. Position the left upward palm in front of you at the same time when the right "G" hand is placed upwardly. Now bring the right "G" hand, palm facing left, to touch the left palm near the wrist and move it straight in the direction of front right diagonal across the left open hand, ending the right hand motion beyond the fingertips of the left hand.

# GOSPEL

Teachings of Jesus and the Apostles; any one of the first four books of the New Testament; "Good News."

Rub the left open upward palm with the right "G" hand, palm facing left and the back edge nearest the little finger of the "G" hand brushing the left palm at least twice.

# GRACE

Unmerited favor of God; favor and love of God.

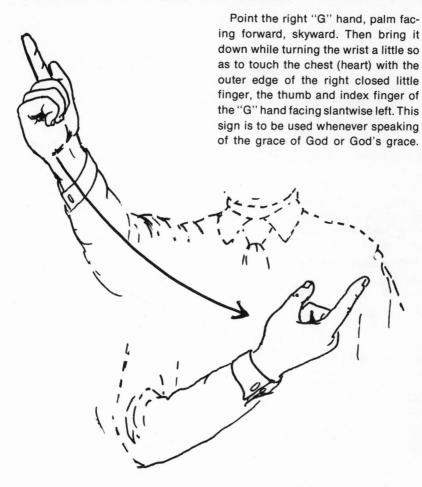

Point the right "G" hand, palm facing forward, skyward. Then bring it down while turning the wrist a little so as to touch the chest (heart) with the outer edge of the right closed little finger, the thumb and index finger of the "G" hand facing slantwise left. This sign is to be used whenever speaking of the grace of God or God's grace.

# GRAVE

Hole dug in the ground where a dead body is to be buried; any place of burial.

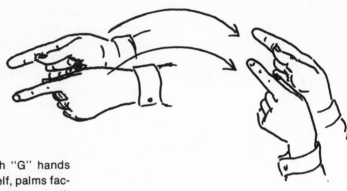

Place both "G" hands in front of self, palms facing down. Move both hands back toward self in a rearward and downward arc.

# GUILTY

Having done wrong; deserving to be blamed and punished; knowing or showing that one has done wrong.

Tap the chest or heart area with the right "G" hand at least twice, the outer edge of the thumb and index finger touching.

76

# HEAVEN

Place where God and the angels live; place of greatest happiness.

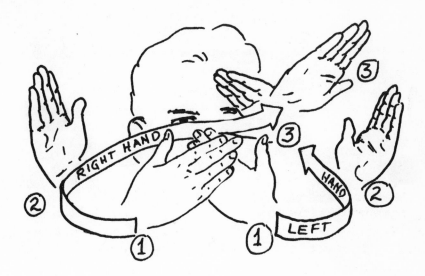

Using both open hands, palms facing in, bring them around in a circle toward self and then pass the right open hand under the left hand and up. This motion is made slightly above eye level.

# HEBREW

Jew; the ancient language of the Jews.

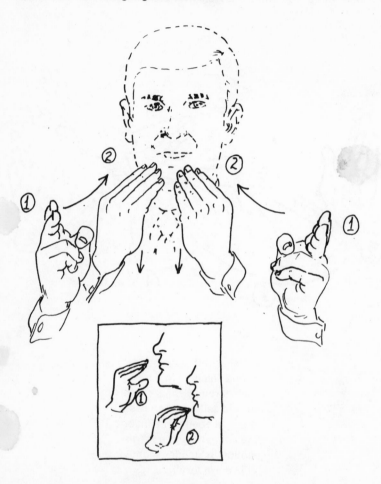

With both hands in the "H" position, palms facing each other, place them in front of self and move them in a very slight downward quarter arc toward each other. Then stroke the chin with both hands, the fingertips of each hand brushing the chin and then touching the thumb as if you are stroking a beard.

# HELL

Place where wicked persons are punished after death; any place of wickedness.

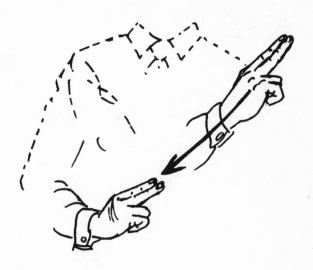

Move the right "H" hand, the tips of the index and middle fingers pointing forward, from the front center midair area straight down to the right side at the waist or thigh area, the hand still being in the "H" position.

# HOLY SPIRIT

Spirit of God.

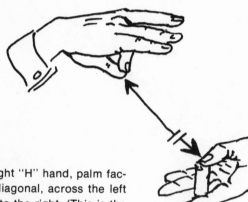

Move the right "H" hand, palm facing rear left diagonal, across the left upward palm to the right. (This is the sign for "holy.") Then bring the tips of the middle finger and thumb of the right hand, palm facing downward, to touch the tips of the middle finger and thumb of the left hand, palm facing upward. Now move both hands away from each other in a slightly vertical direction, the right hand moving farther up while the left hand is lowered a little bit.

## HOSANNA

Shout of praise to the Lord.

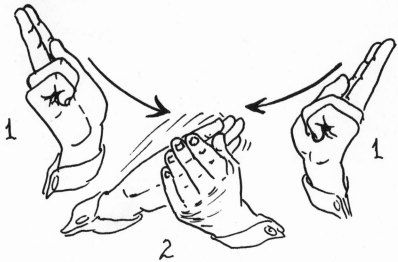

Place the right "H" hand slightly above and to the right of the left "H" hand, palms facing each other. Move both hands toward each other and then open them to flat palms facing each other. Now clap the hands at least twice to convey the idea of praise to God.

## HYMN

Song in praise or honor of God; any song of praise.

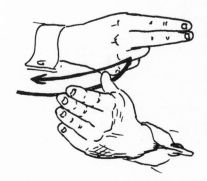

Swing the right "H" hand, palm facing rear left diagonal, back and forth across the left upward palm.

# HYPOCRITE

Person who pretends to be what he is not.

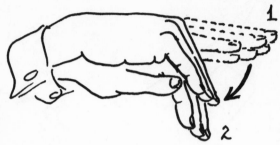

Place the palm of the right hand on the back of the left hand and then bend both hands downward slightly toward self.

# IDOL

Image or other object worshiped as a god.

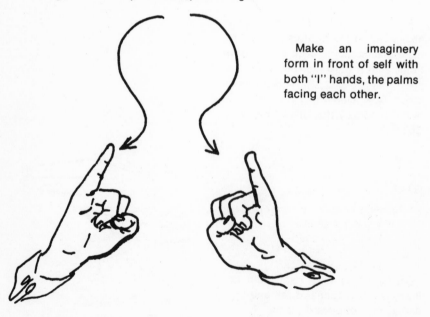

Make an imaginery form in front of self with both "I" hands, the palms facing each other.

# IMMORTAL (ITY)

Never dying; everlasting.

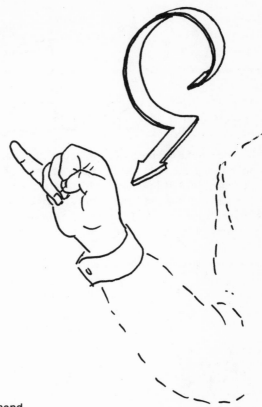

Move the right "I" hand, palm facing forward, in a clockwise and then forward motion, still retaining the "I." This is the same as the sign for "forever," except the letter here is "I."

## INCARNATE (ION)

Embodied in human form or flesh.

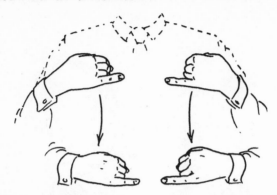

With both hands in the "I" position, palms facing self tap the right chest with the right hand and at the same time the left chest with the left hand. Move both hands slightly away from the body in a downward motion only to touch the waist area. This is the same as the sign for "body," except the hands are in the "I." This conveys the idea of being embodied in human form or flesh.

## INFINITE

Without limits; extremely great.

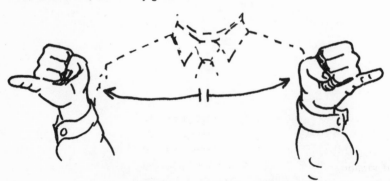

With both hands in the "I" position, palms facing each other, place the hands at least two or three inches apart. Move both hands in the opposite horizonal direction to magnify "extreme greatness."

84

## INSPIRE (ATION)

Put thought, feeling, life, force into; breathe in; influence; affect.

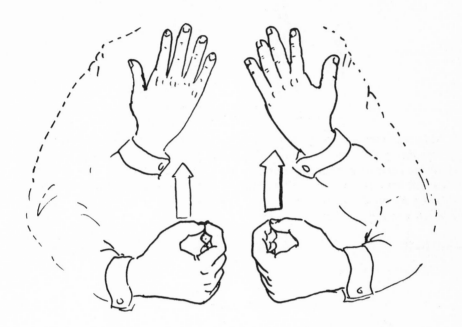

With both hands in the nearly flattened "O" position, palms facing self, place them at the waist area. Move them upward across the chest while opening them into a spread fashion.

# INTERPRET (ATION) (ER)

Bring out or explain the meaning of.

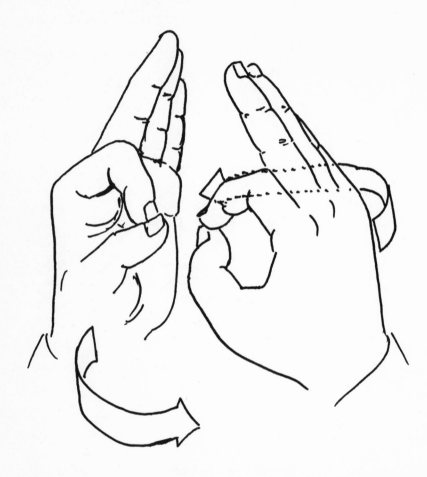

With both hands in the "F" position, palms slightly slanted and facing each other, move the right hand in a forward, semicircular motion while the left hand is turned in a backward semicircular motion. Add the sign for "-tion" to signify "interpretation." Add the sign for "-er" to indicate an "interpreter."

# ISRAEL

Jews; Hebrews; ancient kingdom in north Palestine.

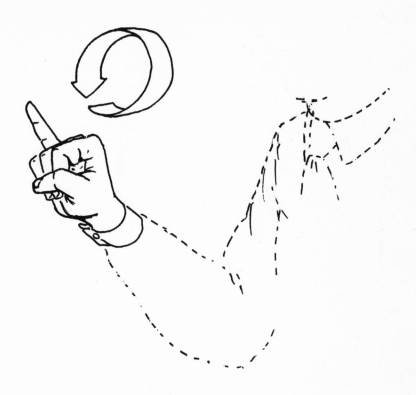

Move the right "I" hand, palm facing forward, in a clockwise circle in front of self.

# JERUSALEM

Capital of Israel.

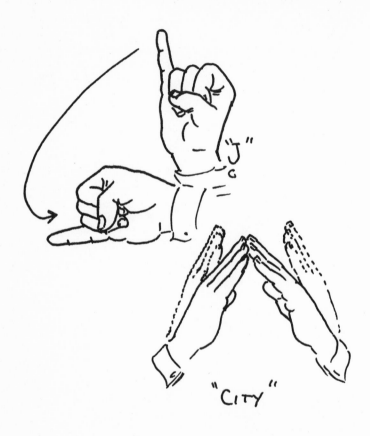

"J"

"CITY"

Make the letter "J" with the right hand, followed immediately by the touch of the fingertips of both hands, palms facing each other and the wrists being at least several inches apart. In a rapid motion move the fingers away from each other and then back to touch again while keeping the wrists in almost the same position.

## JESUS

Founder of Christian religion.

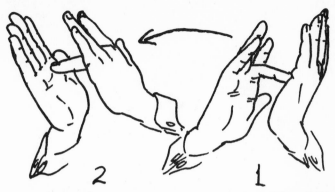

Touch the left open palm, which is facing right, with the middle finger of the right hand, which is facing left. Then touch the right open palm with the middle finger of the left hand, palm facing right. This denotes the idea of pierced hands.

## JEW (ISH)

Member of people that formerly lived in Palestine but now live in many countries; person whose religion is Judaism.

When using just your right hand, stroke the chin with it, the palm facing self and the thumb facing the fingers. At almost the end of the downward motion, have the thumb touch the fingers (most likely the index and middle fingers). When both hands are used, stroke the right hand and the left part with the left hand in a manner similar to the motion of the right hand.

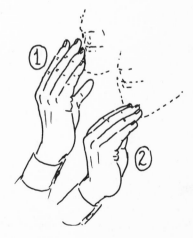

# KINGDOM

Country that is governed by a king or queen; rule or realm of God.

Touch the left shoulder with the right "K" hand, palm facing self. Bring it down to touch the right side of the waist. Then change the hand from "K" into an open downward palm and move it over the left arm in a semi-counterclockwise arc, while at the same time position the left bent arm before you.

90

## LAMB OF GOD

Christ pictured as a lamb slain for man's sin.

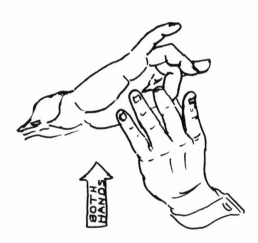

Rub across the back of the slightly bent left arm, the palm facing downward, with the right "K" hand, the palm facing upward. (This indicates the idea of the sheep being sheared.) Then position the left hand in midair in front of self, palm facing upward and the tips of the thumb and index finger touching and forming a ring with the tips of the left thumb and index finger inside of it (ring). Now move both hands upward. (This is the sign for "of.") Drop the left hand while moving the right "B" hand upward at eye level, palm facing left. Bring the right hand back and then down. (Actually, this motion contains three signs: "Lamb," "of" and "God.")

## LAW

Rule made by a king, country or God; a system of rules.

Place the right "L" hand against the left open hand, both palms facing forward but slanted differently.

## LAYMAN

Person outside of any particular profession—not belonging to clergy.

Touch the right forehead with the right "L" hand, palm facing self. While moving the right hand in a forward horizonal motion, change the letter sign into a sign for "man," the inside edges of all the fingers pressed together and the thumb touching the index and middle fingers, palm facing downward.

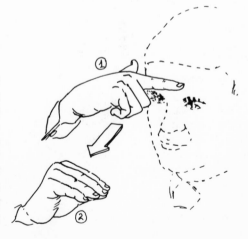

## LEGAL (ISM)

Strict adherence to law.

Position the left flat palm facing front right diagonal in front of self, all the fingers pointing skyward. Strike the left finger area with the edge of the right "L" hand, palm facing front left diagonal. In a rapid succession, move the right hand at least an inch or two away from the left hand and then down while changing from "L" to "G." End the motion with the right "G" hand on the left palm.

## LIFE

Living; being alive.

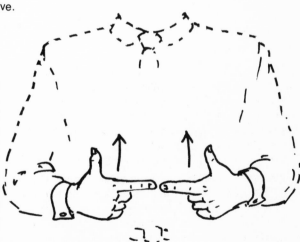

With both hands in the "L" position, place the right hand at the right side of the waist level and the left hand in a similar left position, both palms facing self. Bring the hands upward across the chest.

# LONGING

Earnest desire.

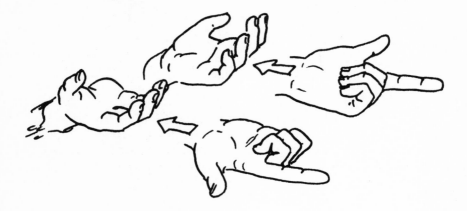

Place both "L" hands, palms upward, in front of self. Bring both hands toward self while changing the letters from "L" to "C." (The "C" is in a finger-spread fashion.) Having done so, move the hands forward and backward while bending and unbending the fingers of both hands slightly.

# LORD

Owner, ruler, or master; God.

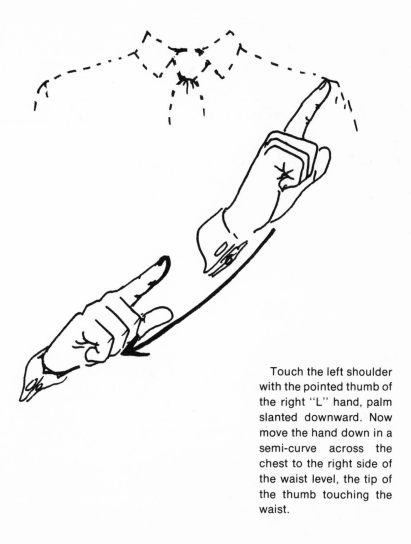

Touch the left shoulder with the pointed thumb of the right "L" hand, palm slanted downward. Now move the hand down in a semi-curve across the chest to the right side of the waist level, the tip of the thumb touching the waist.

## LOYAL (TY)

Faithful to love, promise, or duty; faithful to one's church, country, or government; faithful to God.

Place the left "L" hand in front of self, the palm slanted toward self. At the same time place the right "S" hand, palm facing self, below and to the right of the left "L" hand. Now strike the lower edge of the left hand with the clenched fingers of the right hand, both palms still facing self.

# LORD'S SUPPER

Jesus' last supper with his disciples; church service in memory of Jesus' last supper with his disciples.

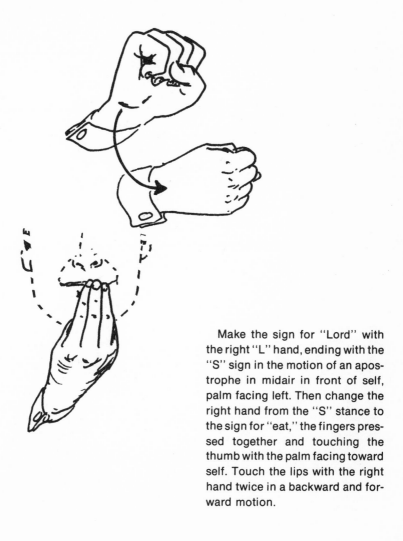

Make the sign for "Lord" with the right "L" hand, ending with the "S" sign in the motion of an apostrophe in midair in front of self, palm facing left. Then change the right hand from the "S" stance to the sign for "eat," the fingers pressed together and touching the thumb with the palm facing toward self. Touch the lips with the right hand twice in a backward and forward motion.

# MAGNIFY

Cause to be or look larger.

Praise: position the left open upward palm in front of self. Now clap the left hand with the first three fingers of the right "M" hand.

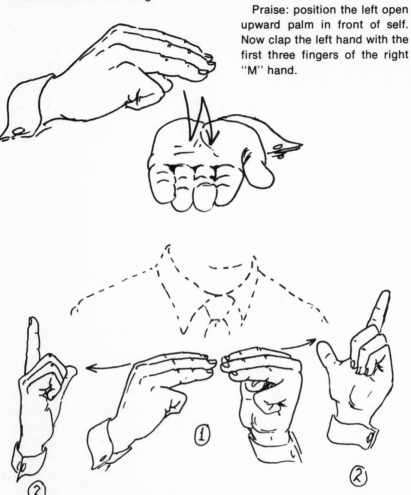

Look larger: bring to touch the fingertips of both "M" hands, palms facing slantwise toward self. While moving both hands away from each other, change the letters from "M" to "L" to signify "large."

## MAJESTY

Grandeur; dignity; stateliness.

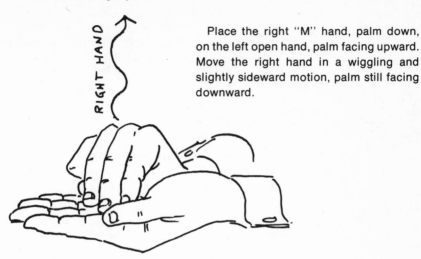

Place the right "M" hand, palm down, on the left open hand, palm facing upward. Move the right hand in a wiggling and slightly sideward motion, palm still facing downward.

## MANIFEST (ATION)

Show plainly; prove.

Place the right "M" hand, palm facing left, on the left open hand, palm facing front right diagonal. Move both hands forward. It is the same as the sign for "show," except the right hand is in the "M" position.

## MASTER

Person who rules or commands people; the one in control.

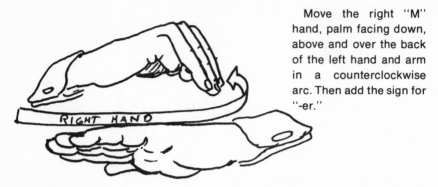

Move the right "M" hand, palm facing down, above and over the back of the left hand and arm in a counterclockwise arc. Then add the sign for "-er."

## MATERIAL (ISM)

Belief that all action, thought, and feeling can be explained by movements and changes in matter; tendency to care too much for the things of this world.

Position the left "M" hand, palm slanted down and toward self, in midair in front of self. Touch the top of the left "M" hand with the bottom of the right "M" hand. Now move both "M" hands, each coming into play by itself, in a clockwise circle, ending the motion with the right hand again on top of the left hand. It is the same as the sign for "world," except for the "M" position.

## MATURE (ITY)

Ripe; full grown; carefully thought out.

Position the left "S" hand in front midair, palm facing right. At the same time place the right "M" hand, palm facing downward, to the right of the left hand. Now move the right hand to the left across the left hand.

## MEDITATE (ION)

Think about; consider.

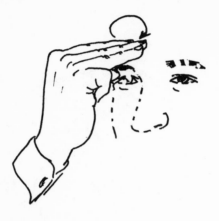

Place the right "M" at eye level, the fingers being near the right side of the forehead. Move it in a small circle. It is the same as the sign for "think," the right hand being in the "M" position.

# MEDIATOR

Be a connecting link; person who settles by intervening or bringing about an agreement between persons or things.

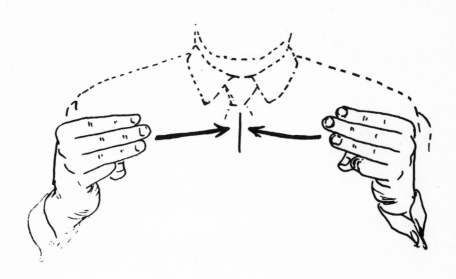

With both hands in the "M" position and the fingers pointing in a slanted forward direction, the palms facing each other, bring them together to the touching point of the "M" fingers. Then add the sign for "-er." (This conveys the idea of the person being the meeting point for two opposing parties or being responsible for seeking reconciliation between persons by bringing them together to settle their differences.)

# MEMORIAL

Something that is a reminder of some great event or person; helping to remember.

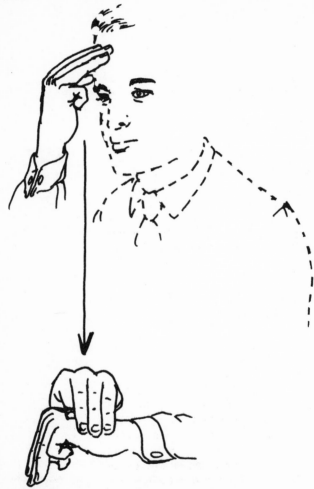

Touch the right center of the forehead with the right "M" hand, palm facing self, while the left "M" hand, palm down, is positioned in front of you. Bring the right hand, palm down, to rest on the back of the left hand, the first three right "M" fingers touching.

# MERCY

More kindness than justice requires; in the power of.

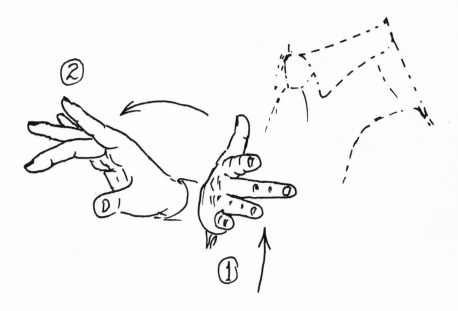

Touch the heart with the right middle finger, the thumb and other fingers being extended. Rub the heart area a few inches upwardly and turn the hand so as to bring the palm to face forward, still using the middle finger and having the thumb and other fingers extended. Move it in a forward circle and a half.

# MERIT

Goodness, worth or value; thing that deserves praise or reward; real fact or quality, whether good or bad.

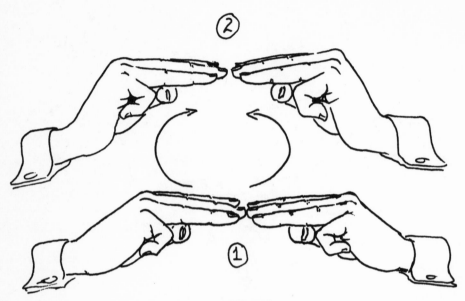

With both hands in the "M" position, palms facing each other, bring to touch the fingertips of both hands. Move the right hand in an upward half circle and at the same time the left hand in the left similar motion. End the cycle with the fingertips of both hands contacting again. It is the same as the sign for "worth," "value," et cetera.

## MINISTER

Be helpful; give aid; contribute. Clergyman serving a church.

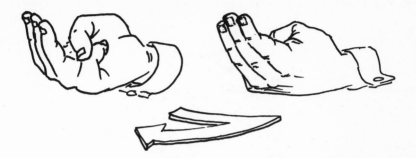

Verb: With the hands in the "M" position, palms facing upward, move both hands to the left and then to the right. It is the same as the sign for "serve," except that the hands are in the "M" stance.

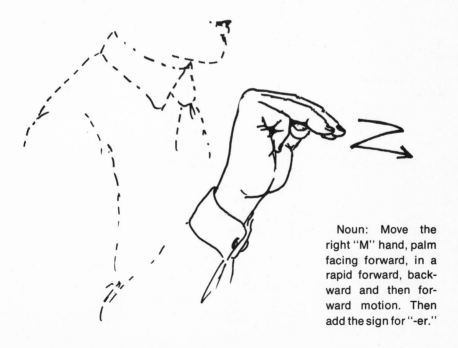

Noun: Move the right "M" hand, palm facing forward, in a rapid forward, backward and then forward motion. Then add the sign for "-er."

# MINISTRY

Duties of a minister.

Place the right "M" hand over the back of the left "S" hand, the right wrist touching the back edge of the left hand. Tap the left hand at least twice. It is the same as the sign for "work," except that the right hand is in the "M" position.

Missionary — Add the sign for "-er" to signify a "missionary," which can be used as a new sign to differentiate it from the sign for "moral."

# MIRACLE

Wonderful happening that is above the known laws of nature.

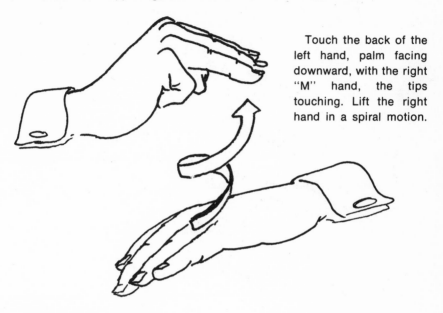

Touch the back of the left hand, palm facing downward, with the right "M" hand, the tips touching. Lift the right hand in a spiral motion.

# MISSION (MISSIONARY)

Sending or being sent on some special work; business or purpose in life or calling; station of a religious mission. Person sent on a religious mission.

Place the right "M" hand, palm facing left, on the left side of the chest (heart area). Move it in a very small clockwise circle while still touching the chest. Add the sign "-er" for "missionary." Also see MINISTRY.

# MORAL (ITY)

Good in character or conduct; capable of understanding right and wrong; having to do with character or with differences between right or wrong.

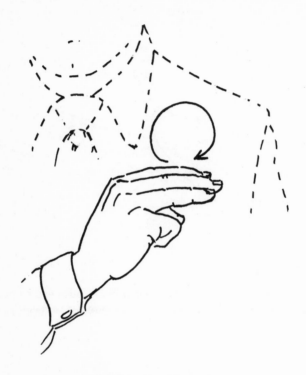

Move the right "M" hand in a large clockwise motion over the left chest or heart area. It is the same as the signs for "character," "personality," "attitude," et cetera, except for the first letter signs.

# MORTAL

Sure to die sometime; deadly; man.

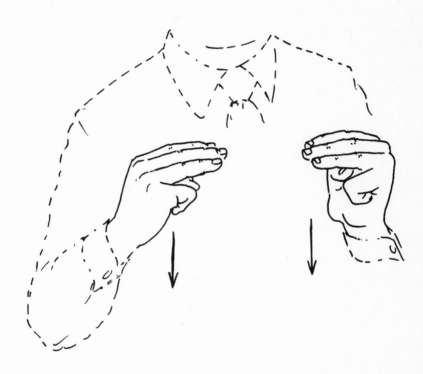

With the hands in the "M" position, the palms facing downward, place them at chest level near self. Move both hands down. It is the same as the sign for "person," except for the "M."

111

# MOTIVE

Thought or feeling that makes one act.

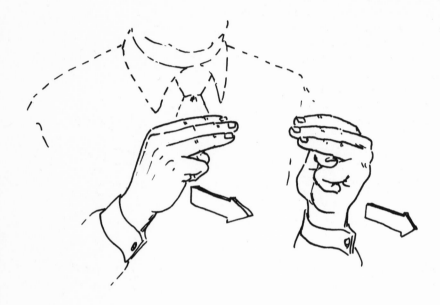

Place both "M" hands in front of self
at the chest level, palms facing each
other. Move both hands forward.

## MOURN

Grieve; feel or show sorrow over.

Rub the heart area with the middle finger of the right hand, other fingers being extended, while at the same time hold the left hand in a semi-clenched (closed) position, palm facing upward, slightly below the right hand. Then bring the right hand down in a semi-closed position, palm facing downward. When the fingers of both hands touch, twist the hands together in the "A" position. This is the same as the sign for "grief."

## MUSIC

Art of getting the sounds together in beautiful or pleasing arrangements.

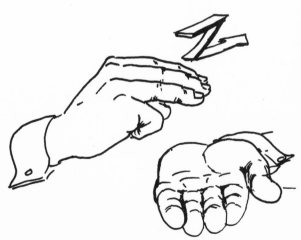

Place the left upward open palm in front of self. Place the right "M" hand, palm facing downward, above and over the fingertips of the left hand. Then swing the right hand back and forth across the left palm and arm.

## MYSTERY

Secret; something hidden or unknown.

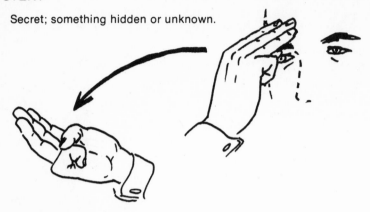

Touch the right forehead with the fingertips of the right "M" hand. Move the hand away from the forehead to the right, still retaining the "M" position, similar to the sign for "don't know."

## MYTH

Legend or story; any invented story; imaginary person or thing.

Touch the right forehead with the fingertips of the right "M" hand. Let the right "M" hand hop twice in a forward motion, palm still facing left.

## NATURE

The world; all things except those made by man. Quality or character.

When speaking of "character" or man's "nature," use this sign: make a large clockwise circle over the heart area with the right "N" hand.

When speaking of the world of nature, use the following sign: position the left "N" hand in front of self, the palm slanted downward and toward self. Touch the top of the left "N" hand with the bottom of the right "N" hand in a similar 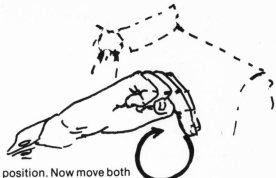 position. Now move both "N" hands, each coming into play by itself, in a clockwise circle, ending the motion with the right hand again on top of the left hand. This is the same as the sign for "world," except for the "N" stance.

# NEIGHBOR

One who lives near another.

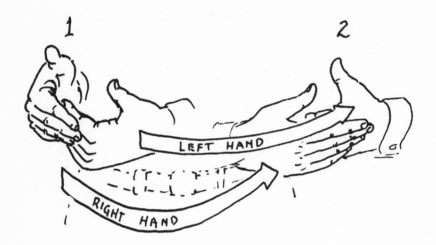

1    2

LEFT HAND

RIGHT HAND

Place the left open hand, palm facing self, near the right wrist area. Touch the back of the left hand with the palm of the right hand. Then move the right hand very slightly away from the left hand and to the left while the left hand is moved in a barely visible arc to the left waist. Have the right palm touch the back of the left hand again at the end of the leftward movement. Add the sign for "-er."

# OATH

Solemn promise.

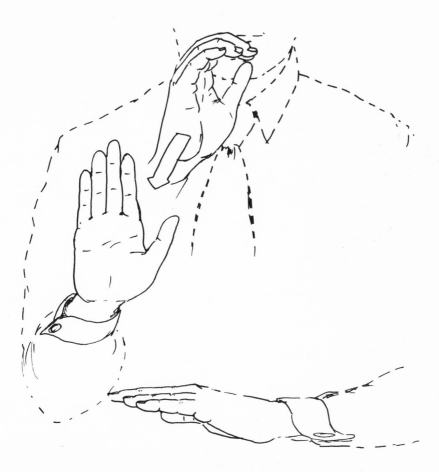

Touch the lips with the right "O" hand, palm facing left. Then move the hand away from the lips to the right while opening it to a flat upraised position, palm facing forward. While the right hand is being raised, touch the right elbow with the outer edge of the index finger of the left hand, palm facing down.

Use the "V" sign at the outset for "vow." Retain the original index finger movement for "swear."

## OBSERVE

See and note; examine and study; keep or follow in practice.

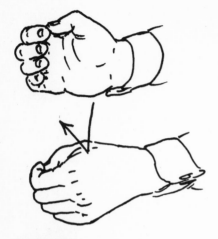

With both hands in the "O" position, place the right hand above and over the left hand. Tap both hands once or twice, the edge of the palm of the right "O" hand touching the back area below the sides of the thumb and index finger of the left "O" hand. (This sign is to be used whenever the "keeping" idea is indicated such as "observe the Lord's Supper.")

## OCCASION

Particular time; special event; cause or reason.

Move the right "O" hand, palm down, in a small circle over the left open upward palm in front of self. Then land the right "O" hand on the left hand, the back edge of the "O" thumb touching.

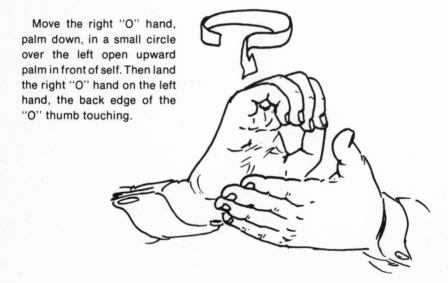

118

# OFFER

Hold out to be taken or refused; give something as an act of worship; present in worship.

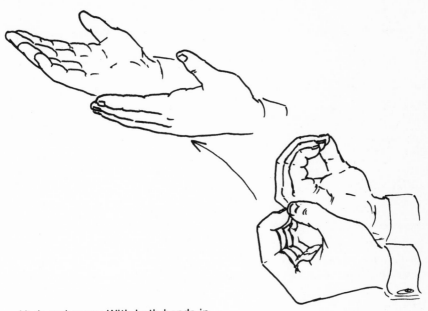

Verb and noun: With both hands in the "O" position, palms upward, bring the hands upward while opening them into flat upward palms as if making a sign for "offer."

## OFFERING

Collection or giving money to a church.

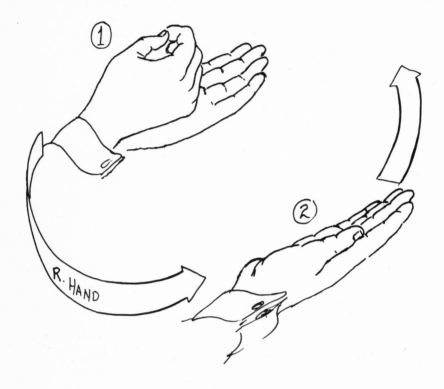

R. HAND

Offering such as money: With the right "O" hand, palm facing left, touch the left flat upward palm once. In a rapid succession, change the right "O" hand into a flat upward palm and move it beyond the stationary left hand in a semi-counterclockwise motion as if passing out a collection plate.

## OMNIPOTENT

Almighty.

Touch the left shoulder with the right "O" hand, palm facing downward, and bring it down to touch the left arm below and near the elbow joint, similar to the sign for "power."

## OMNIPRESENT

Present everywhere.

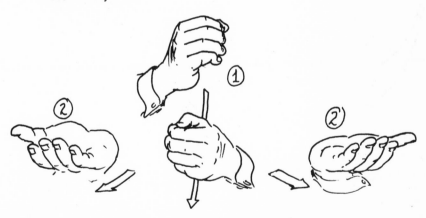

Place the left "O" hand, palm facing right, in front of self. Brush vertically the back of the thumb of the left "O" hand with the right "O" hand, palm facing left. Then move the right "O" hand to the right and the left "O" hand to the left, while changing them into flat upward palms. It is the same as the sign for "everywhere," except that the hands are in the "O" position at the outset.

121

# OMNISCIENT

Knowing everything.

Touch the right forehead with the fingertips of the right "O" hand, palm facing downward. With the left "O" hand, palm facing right, in front of self, brush once downwardly the back of the left "O" thumb with the outer part of the right "O" fingers. While the left hand is held in the same position, open the right hand, palm facing upward, at the end of its downward motion and then move to the right, palm still in a flat upward position. This motion indicates the idea of knowing everything.

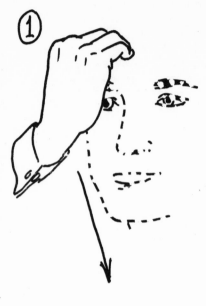

# OPPORTUNITY

A good chance; favorable time.

With both hands in the "O" position, palms facing downward, place them in midair in front of self. Flip the wrists upward while changing from "O" to "P," the palms facing forward.

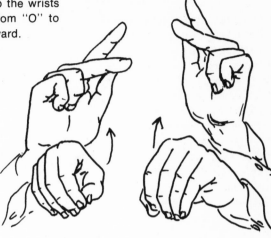

# ORDINANCE

Rule or law made by authority; decree.

With the left flat palm facing front right diagonal, the fingers pointing up, touch the left finger area with the outer edge of the thumb and index finger of the right "O" hand, palm facing front left diagonal. Bring the right "O" hand down in a very slight curve to touch the palm area of the left hand.

# ORGANIZATION

Group of persons united for some purpose.

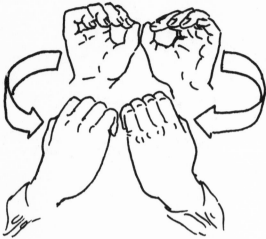

With the hands in the "O" position, bring to touch the outer sides of the thumbs and index fingers of both hands, palms facing forward. Then move the right hand in a right semicircle and at the same time the left hand in a similar left motion. With the hands in a forward circle movement, bring to touch the outer sides of the little fingers and palms of the "O" hands, palms now facing self.

# OWN

Possess; admit; confess. Of oneself or itself.

With both hands in the "O" position and several inches away from the chest in front of self, touch the chest with the fingertips of the hands. It is the same as the sign for "have," except that the hands are in the "O" stance.

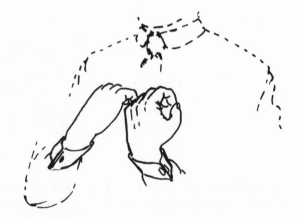

# PARABLE

Short story used to teach some lesson or truth.

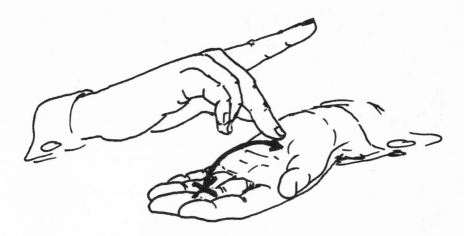

Place the tip of the middle finger of the right "P" hand on the finger area of the left open upward palm. Move the right "P" hand in a slight backward semi-curve, ending with the middle finger touching the left palm area.

# PARDON

Forgive; excuse; set free from punishment.

Brush at least twice the finger area of the left open upward palm with the fingers of the right open hand, palm facing downward.

## PASSION

Very strong feeling; love between a man and a woman.

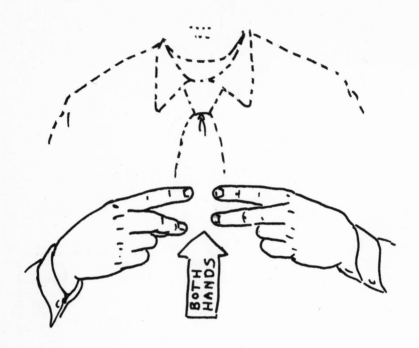

Rub the chest upwardly with both "P" hands, the middle fingertips touching and both palms facing self.

# PASSOVER

Annual feast of the Jews.

SIDE VIEW

Tap the left elbow with the right "P" hand, the palm facing down and the thumb and the index and middle fingers touching.

## PATRIARCH

Father and ruler of a family or tribe; venerable old man.

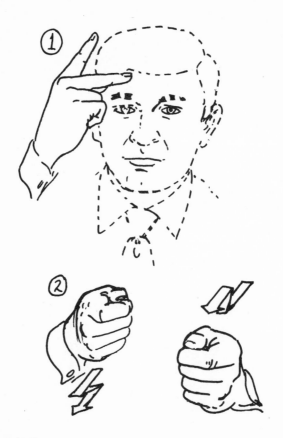

Touch the right side of the forehead with the middle fingertip of the right "P" hand, palm facing self. Bring it down while changing from "P" to the "holding the (stagecoach) horse rein" position. At the same time place the left hand in a similar position. Then move the right hand forward and backward while doing the same with the left hand in the opposite direction. Add the sign for "-er." This is the same as the signs for "male parent" and "ruler."

## PEACE

Freedom from war or strife of any kind; public quiet, order and security.

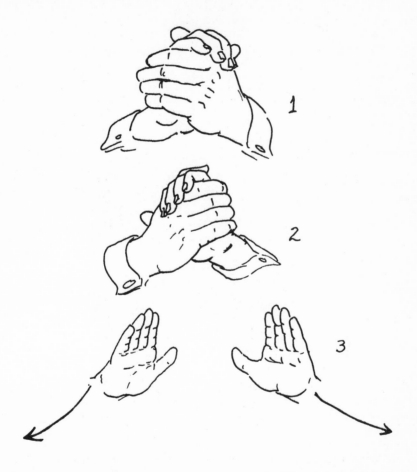

Hold the hands together in the position of a clasp, the right hand being upper and the left hand being lower. Unclasp the hands and turn both wrists to the right. Then hold the hands again, the left hand being upper this time. Follow immediately with the near contact of the index fingers and thumbs of both hands which swing down in the opposite curves.

129

# PENALTY

Punishment.

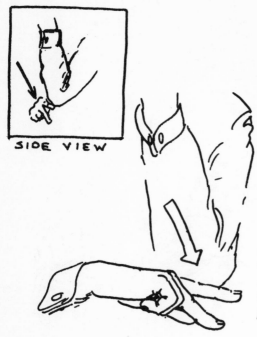

SIDE VIEW

Brush the left elbow with the right "P" hand, palm facing self, in a downward motion. This is used whenever the idea of punishment for sin is expressed. For example: "The *penalty* of sin is death."

Penalize, fine, et cetera: Strike down across the left open hand, palm facing rear right diagonal, with the tip of the middle finger of the right "P" hand. It is the same as the sign for "fine," "charge," et cetera, as well as for "marking a demerit," except that the right hand is in the "P" position.

130

# PERSONAL

Individual; done in a person.

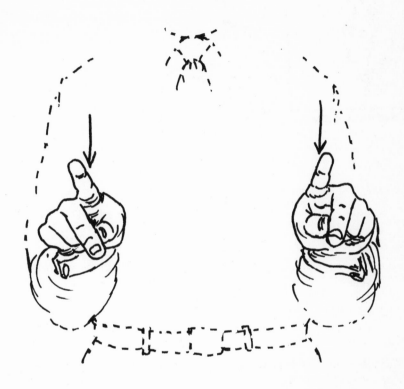

With the hands in the "P" position
and at the sides of the body, bring both
hands down, the palms facing downward.

## PERSONALITY

The personal quality that makes one person be different or act differently from another.

Place the right "P" hand, palm facing down at a slant, near the heart area. Move it in a large clockwise circle. Then touch the chest with the thumb and middle finger of the right "P" hand.

## PHARISEE

Member of an ancient Jewish sect that was very strict in keeping to the laws of its religion.

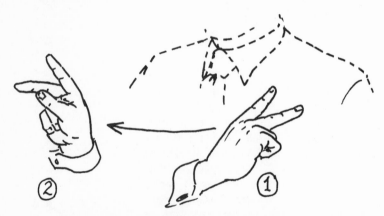

Touch the heart area with the middle fingertip of the right "P" hand, palm facing self. Swing it in a forward and upward arc until the palm of the right "P" hand faces slightly forward. Add the sign for "-er." This denotes the idea of a person being a strict adherent of religion.

## PLEAD

Ask earnestly; speak for or against; argue.

Position the left open hand in front of self, palm facing right. Touch the left palm with the right "P" hand, palm facing forward. Move both hands backward. It is the same as the sign for "ask," except the right hand is in the "P" position.

# PLEDGE

A solemn promise; give as security.

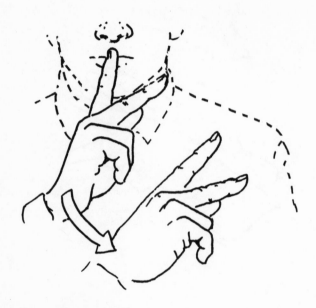

Touch the lips with the side of the index finger of the right "P" hand, palm facing to the left. Then move it down to touch the heart area, palm facing down and the thumb and the index and middle fingers touching.

# PRIEST

Jewish religious leader performing a priestly function in ancient Israel; a clergyman of a Christian church.

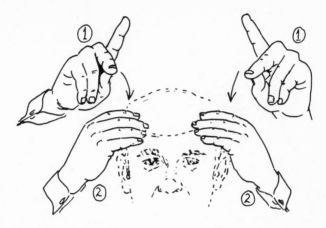

(Jewish) With both hands in the "P" position, palms facing each other, place the hands over the head. Then change from "P" to "C" with the fingers extended while moving both hands slightly down to form a "crown" over the head.

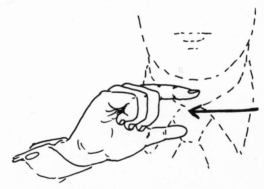

(Catholic) Bring to touch the tips of the thumbs and index fingers of both hands, palms facing each other, at the throat area. Now move both hands away from each other across the throat to signify the white collar worn by a Catholic priest.

135

# PROFESS

Claim; declare openly.

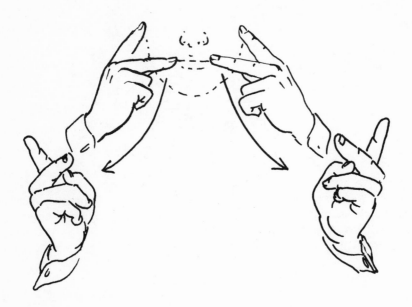

With the hands in the "P" position, touch the lips with the tips of the middle fingers. Move the right "P" hand in a right forward arc and the left "P" hand in a similar left motion. It is the same as the sign for "announce" or "declare," except for the "P's."

# PROGRAM

List of items or events; plan of what is to be done.

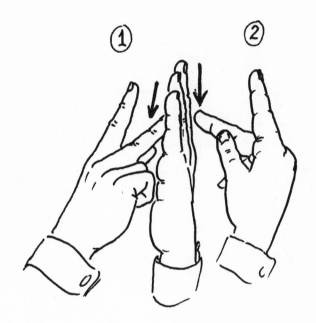

Touch the top of the middle finger of the left open hand with the tip of the middle finger of the right "P" hand, both palms facing each other. Now bring the right "P" hand down vertically across the left palm and then repeat it on the back of the left hand.

# PROPHECY

A foretelling of future events; a divinely inspired utterance.

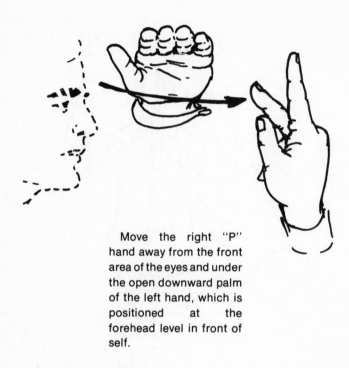

Move the right "P" hand away from the front area of the eyes and under the open downward palm of the left hand, which is positioned at the forehead level in front of self.

# PROPHET

Person who tells what will happen; person who preaches what he thinks has been revealed to him.

Make the sign for "prophecy" and then add the sign for "-er."

138

# PSALM

Sacred song or poem.

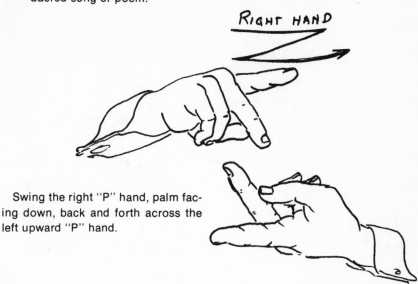

*Right Hand*

Swing the right "P" hand, palm facing down, back and forth across the left upward "P" hand.

# PURE

Perfectly clean; spotless; perfect; with no evil.

*R. Hand*

Move the right "P" hand, palm facing down, across the left upward open palm, the fingers of the left "P" hand facing front right diagonal and the tip of the middle finger of the right "P" hand touching.

## RABBI

Teacher of Jewish religion; pastor of Jewish congregation.

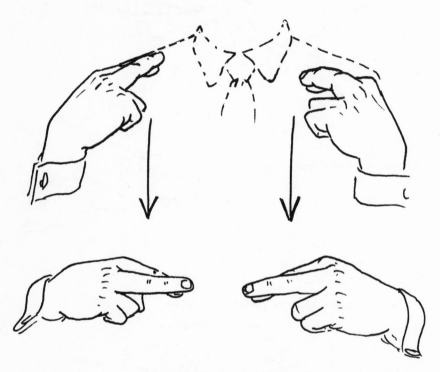

With the hands in the "R" position and resting on the front edge of the shoulders, move both hands downward to indicate a sash worn by the rabbi.

# RACE

Group of people.

With the hands in the "R" position, bring to touch the sides of the hands, palms facing forward. Move the right hand in a forward right semicircle and the left hand in a similar left motion, ending with the sides of the hands touching, the palms now facing self. This sign is used to indicate a race of people.

# RANSOM

Price paid or demanded before a captive is set free.

Position the left "R" hand, palm facing rear right diagonal, in front of self. Place the right "R" hand, palm facing rear left diagonal, on top of the left hand. Now move the right hand backward, downward, under and forward of the left hand. At the same time move the left hand upward and backward. The idea is to indicate the *exchange* of money for a person held for ransom.

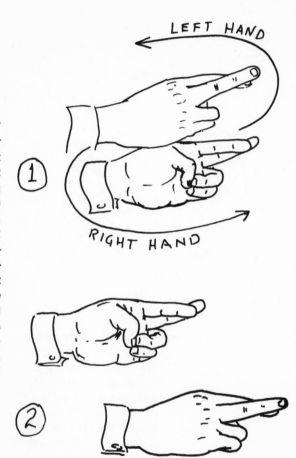

LEFT HAND

RIGHT HAND

## REBEL (LION)

Resist authority; oppose; feel a great dislike.

Touch the forehead with the right "R" hand, the tips of the index and middle fingers touching. Then twist the right hand to the right while changing from "R" to "S" in motion. It is the same as the sign for "disobey," except that the "R" is used at the outset of the motion.

## RECONCILE (ATION)

Make friends again; make agree; make satisfaction.

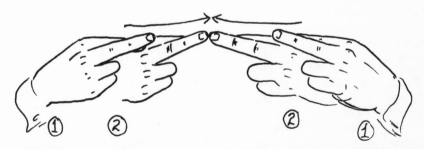

With the hands in the "R" position, the palms facing slightly upward and the "R" fingers pointing slightly forward, bring to touch the tips of both "R" fingers. This conveys the idea of Jesus bringing God and man to meet together on friendly terms, i.e. "He reconciled us to God."

## REDEEM (ER) (EMPTION)

Buy back; pay off; set free.

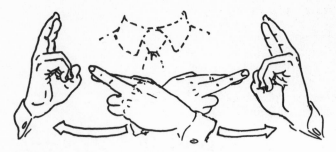

Place the left "R" hand, palm facing right, in front of self and the right "R" hand, palm facing left, on top of the left hand, the wrists of both hands touching. Move both hands away from each other in the opposite horizonal direction. Add the sign "-tion" for "redemption."

Add the sign "-er" for "redeemer." This sign is to be used in Protestant and Catholic services. It is omitted in the Jewish services. The Jewish worshipers use the same sign for both "redeem" and "redeemer."

## REFORM (ATION)

Make or become better; improve; changing one's manner of life, conduct, et cetera, for the better.

Place in front of self the wrist of the right "R" hand, palm facing downward, on the wrist of the left "R" hand, palm facing upward. Twist both hands, their "R" fingers pointing forward, to the right so as to bring the left hand to the top and the right hand to the bottom. This conveys the outward change of a person's life, et cetera.

144

## REFUSE (AL)

Decline to accept; reject.

Place the right "S" hand with the thumb opening at the right side before self. Draw it backward toward the shoulder.

# RELIGION

Belief in God or gods; worship of God or gods.

# RELIGIOUS

Very much interested in religion.

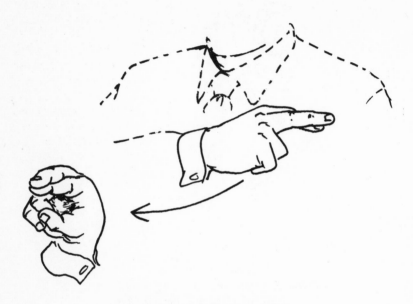

Touch the heart area with the tips of the right "R" fingers, the palm facing self. Twist the hand in a forward and upward arc, ending with the palm facing out and the "R" fingers pointing forward.

## REPENT (ANCE)

Feel sorry for sin and seek forgiveness; regret.

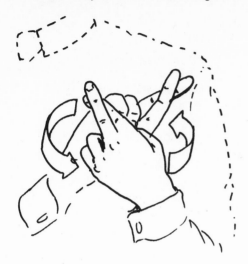

Place near the heart area the right "R" hand on top of the left "R" hand, both palms facing each other and the closed fingers touching. Twist both hands to the right so as to bring the left hand to the top and the right hand to the bottom. This indicates an inner change or a change of the heart.

## REPROVE

Find fault with; rebuke; blame.

Place the right "R" hand in front of self, palm facing left. Move the hand slightly forward and backward several times. It is the same as the sign for "scolding."

147

## REVERE (NT, NCE)

Show a deep respect for, mixed with awe and love.

Place the right "R" hand near the face at eye level and the left "R" hand in front and slightly below to the left of the right hand. Move both hands forward, ending the right hand at chin level away from the face.

## REVIVAL

Awakening or increase of interest in religion.

With the hands in the "R" position, palms facing self, brush the heart area with the "R" fingertips of the right and then the left hand in rotation about two times as the hands are moved in a circular clockwise motion.

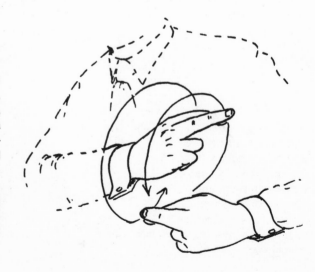

# REVIVE

Make fresh; restore.

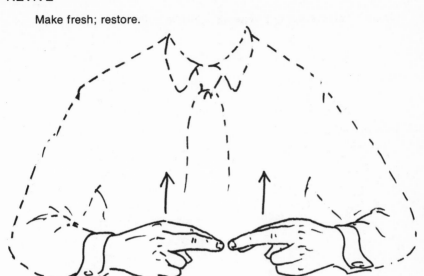

With the hands in the "R" position, place the right hand at the right waist area and the left hand at the left waist area. Move both hands upward across the chest. It conveys the idea of reliving, starting life all over again, or making a fresh start in life again.

# RIGHTEOUS (NESS)

Doing right; behaving justly or properly.

Place the left open upward palm in front of self. Touch the left palm with the tips of the right "R" fingers, palm facing left. Move the right hand across the left palm, the "R" fingers pointing forward. Add the sign for "-ness."

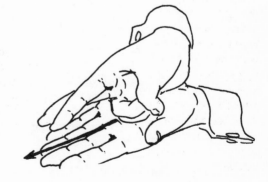

## SABBATH

Jewish holy day that begins at sunset on Friday.

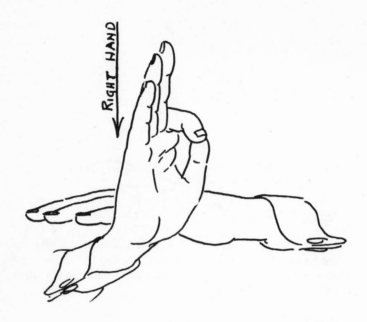

Position the left hand, palm facing down, in front of self. Place the right "F" hand, palm facing left, above and slightly beyond the left hand. Now bring the right "F" hand down while the left hand remains stationary. The "F" stands for a Friday, and the "O" of the thumb and index finger of the "F" symbolizes the sun. The Jewish sabbath begins at a sunset on a Friday.

## SACRIFICE

Act of offering to God or a god; giving up one thing for another.

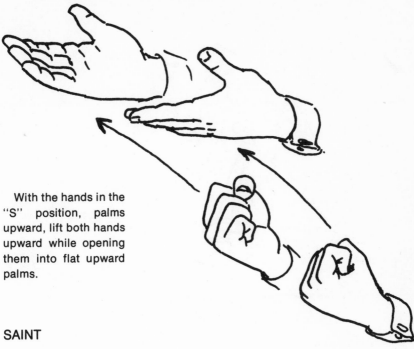

With the hands in the "S" position, palms upward, lift both hands upward while opening them into flat upward palms.

## SAINT

Very holy person.

Place the left upward palm in front of you. Touch the left palm near the wrist with the right "S" hand, palm down. Move the right hand across the left hand, ending slightly beyond the tip of the middle finger. Then add the sign for "-er."

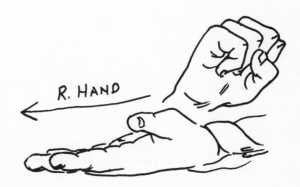

R. HAND

# SAKE

Cause; purpose; because of; to help or please.

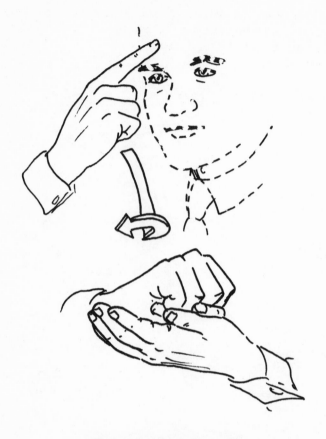

Touch the forehead with the right index finger while placing the left upward open palm in front of self. Bring the right hand down to rest on the left palm while changing the hand in motion to an "S" position. It is the same as the sign for "purpose."

## SANCTIFY (ICATION)

Set apart as sacred.

Place the left upward palm in front of you. Touch the left palm near the wrist with the right "S" hand, palm facing downward. Move the right hand across the left hand, ending slightly beyond the tip of the middle finger. (See "saint.")

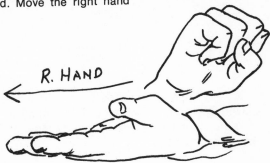

R. HAND

## SANCTUARY

Sacred place; part of the church around the altar.

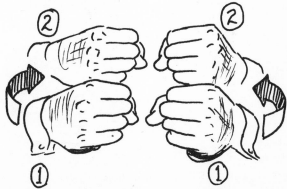

With the hands in the "S" position, the palms facing each other, bring to touch the thumbs of both closed hands in front of self. Move the right hand in a right semicircular motion toward self and the left hand in a similar left motion, ending with the thumbs touching again. This conveys the idea of a sacred *place*.

# SALVATION (SAVE)

A saving of the soul; deliverance from sin.

With both hands in the "S" position, place the right hand, palm facing left, on top of the left hand, palm facing right—the wrists of both hands touching. Move both hands away from each other in the opposite horizonal direction. Add the sign for "-tion."

# SATISFY (ICATION)

To please; make right.

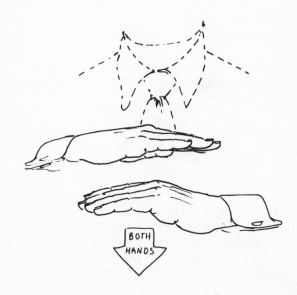

With both hands in the "B" position, the palms facing downward, place the right hand at chest level and the left hand several inches below the right hand. Move both hands down.

## SCRIPTURE

Any sacred writing; (Holy Scriptures) the Bible.

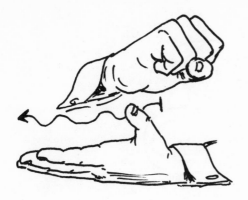

Place the left open upward palm in front of self. Place the right "S" hand, palm facing down, above the left palm near the wrist. Move the right hand across the left palm to the right while shaking it in motion. This indicates a sacred *writing*. If the words "Holy Scriptures" are intended, then these words will be signed in this way: "holy" "scripture," i.e. two signs in one movement.

## SELF-CENTERED

Occupied with one's interests and affairs.

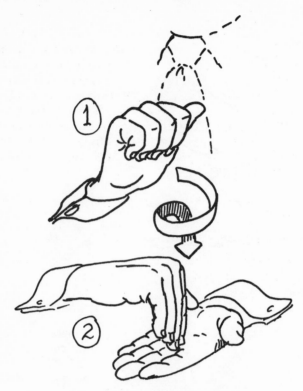

Touch the chest with the right "A" hand, palm facing left and the thumb being extended upward. Place the left open upward palm in front of self. At the same time bring the right hand forward while changing it into a "cupped-hand" position, palm facing downward. Move the right hand in a circular clockwise motion over the left hand, ending with the fingers of the right hand touching the left palm.

## SEMINARY

School or college for training students to be ministers, priests, church leaders, et cetera.

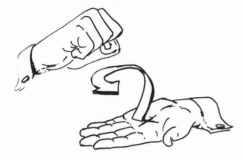

With the left open upward palm being positioned in front of self, touch the left palm with the right "S" hand, palm facing downward. Move the right hand in a left forward arc away from self. It is the same as the sign for "college," except for the "S" position.

## SERVE (SERVICE)

Work for or in; wait on; supply; deliver.

With the open upward palms in front of self, move both hands to the left and then to the right.

BOTH HANDS

## SIN (NER)

Breaking the law of God; wrongdoing of any kind.

 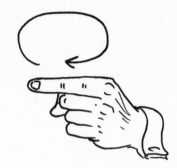

With the index fingers of both hands pointing toward each other, the palms facing self, move both hands in the circles—the right hand in a clockwise motion and the left hand in a counterclockwise motion. Add the sign for "-er."

## SOCIAL

Concerned with human beings as a group; liking company; living or liking to live with others.

With the hands in the "S" position, bring to touch the outer sides of the thumbs and index fingers of both hands, palms facing forward. Move the right hand in a right semicircular motion away from self and the left hand in a similar left motion. While in motion, change the hands from "S" to "L," ending with the outer sides of the little fingers of the "L" hands touching and the palms facing self.

# SOCIETY

Group of persons joined together for a common purpose or by a common interest.

The sign movement is the same as that for "social," except that the hands remain in the "S" position at the end of the motion.

## SPIRIT

Soul; man's moral and religious nature; state of mind or temper.

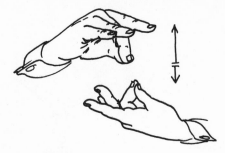

Place in front of self the left upward palm, the tips of the thumb and middle finger being closed but not touched. Do the same with the right hand, the palm facing down and the four fingers of both hands almost intertwining. Move the hands away from each other in a vertical direction, ending with the tips of the thumb and middle finger of each hand touching.

## STEWARD

Man who manages another's property.

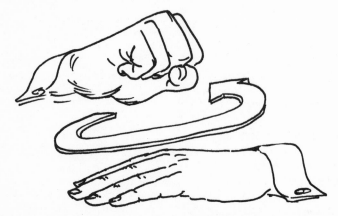

With the right hand in the "S" position, palm facing down, move it away from near the body in a counter-clockwise motion over the back of the left open hand, the palm facing down. Add the sign for "-er."

# STORM (WIND)

Strong wind with rain, snow, hail, or thunder or lightning.

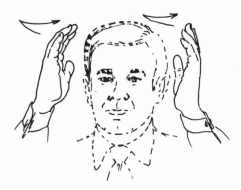

Place both hands in an open, finger-spread fashion in front and above the forehead level, the palms facing each other. Move both hands to the right and then to the left. This sign is used mostly for "wind" but may sometimes be employed for "storm."

Rub across the forehead with the index finger of the right hand, the palm facing self. This is the sign for "black." Place the left upward cupped hand, the fingers slightly spread, in front of self. At the same time bring the right hand, palm down and in a similar position like the left hand, above and around the left hand in a counterclockwise motion. Move simultaneously the left hand but in a smaller counterclockwise direction. The idea here is the wind whirling up a black storm.

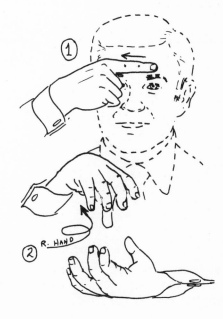

## STRAY

Lose one's way; wander; roam.

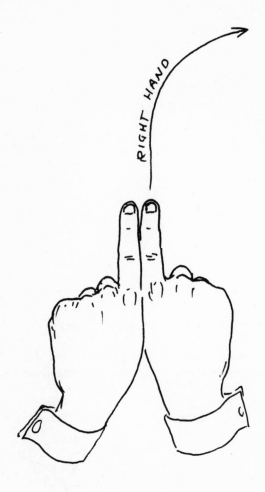

Bring to touch the outer sides
of both index fingers which are
pointing forward. Move the right
hand in a right forward arc.

# STRUGGLE

Try hard; work hard; make great effort with the body.

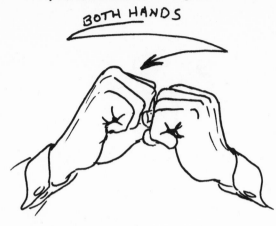

Bring to touch the closed fingers of both "S" hands, the palms facing each other. Move both hands in a quarter arc to the right, then to the left, and again to the right.

# SUBMIT (MISSION)

Yield to the power or control of some person or group.

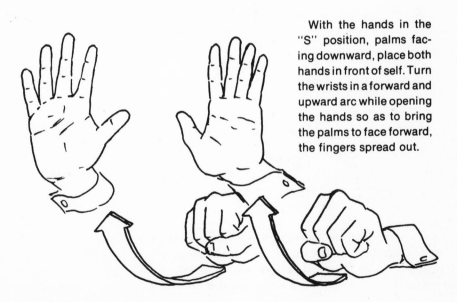

With the hands in the "S" position, palms facing downward, place both hands in front of self. Turn the wrists in a forward and upward arc while opening the hands so as to bring the palms to face forward, the fingers spread out.

## SUBSTANCE

Real, main or important part of anything; matter; material.

With the right hand in the "S" position, the palm facing upward, move it to the right in a jumping or hopping sequences. It is the same as the sign for "thing," except that the right hand is in the "S" stance.

## SUBTLE

Sly; crafty; tricky; having a keen, quick mind.

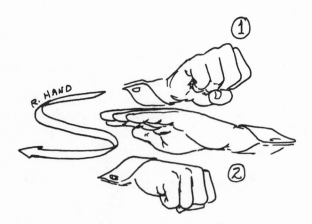

Place the left flat hand, palm down, in front of self. Position the right "S" hand an inch or so above the back of the left hand. Now move the right "S" hand across the left hand and beyond the left fingertips. Bring the right hand back but under the left hand only to move it forward again.

# SUPERSTITION

Unreasoning fear of what is unknown or mysterious; belief or practice founded on ignorant fear.

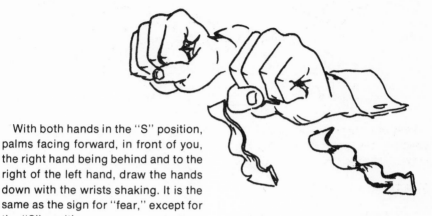

With both hands in the "S" position, palms facing forward, in front of you, the right hand being behind and to the right of the left hand, draw the hands down with the wrists shaking. It is the same as the sign for "fear," except for the "S" position.

## SUPPLICATION

Begging humbly and earnestly.

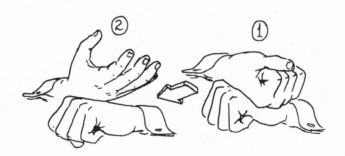

Place the left "S" hand, palm down, in front of self. Position the right "S" hand, palm up, on the back of the left hand. Now open the right hand from the "S" to the cupped position, the palm still upward and the fingers par-tially bent. Draw both hands slightly toward self while bending the right fingers a little further. The sign is similar to the sign for "beg," but this motion begins with the "S" and then "beg" signs.

## SUPPLY

Furnish; provide.

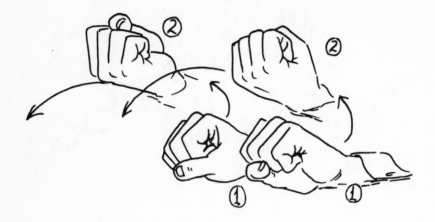

With both hands in the "S" position, the palms facing slightly downward, turn the wrists in a forward and downward arc. This sign is to be used whenever these words are employed: "My God shall *supply* all your needs."

# SYMBOL

Something that stands for or represents something else.

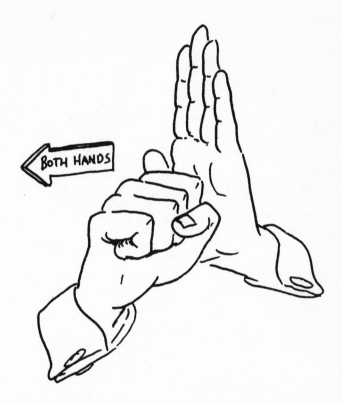

With the left open palm facing front right diagonal and the fingers pointing upward, touch it with the right "S" hand, palm facing front left diagonal. Move both hands forward. This is the same as the sign for "show," except for the "S" position of the right hand.

# TALENT

Special natural ability; gift; aptitude.

Touch the lower part of the left hand, palm facing right, with the right hand, palm facing up and touching the edge of the left hand with the right thumb in contact with the last two left fingers and also with the right fingers in contact with the back of the left hand. Now bring the right hand down while changing it into a "T" position. This sign is to be used whenever speaking of one's talent(s).

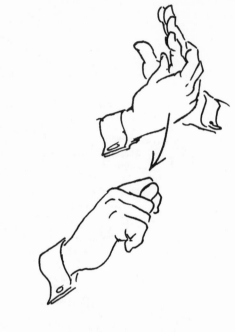

Money in biblical sense: Make a small circle on the left open upward palm with the index finger of the right "T" hand.

# TEMPLE

A building used for service or worship of a god or gods; Jewish or Christian church.

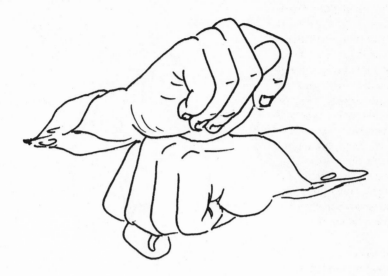

Touch the back of the left "S" hand, palm down, with the right "T" hand, palm down, once or twice.

# TEN COMMANDMENTS

Ten rules for living and worship that God revealed to Moses on Mt. Sinai.

Position the left open hand in front of self, palm facing front right diagonal and the fingers pointing upward. Place the right "A" hand several inches away from the left hand, the thumb of the right hand extending upward and the palm facing front left diagonal. Twist the right hand to the right. In a rapid succession, change the right hand from "A" to "C" in a leftward motion until the right "C" hand touches the left finger area. Then bring the right "C" hand down in a very slight curve to touch the left palm area.

## TESTAMENT (COVENANT)

Law; will; agreement; covenant; a main division of the Bible.

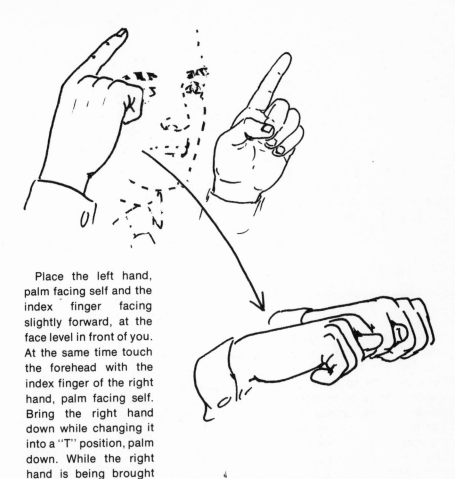

Place the left hand, palm facing self and the index finger facing slightly forward, at the face level in front of you. At the same time touch the forehead with the index finger of the right hand, palm facing self. Bring the right hand down while changing it into a "T" position, palm down. While the right hand is being brought down from the forehead, turn the left hand to the right into a "T" position, palm down. Without stopping to pause, move both "T" hands down a little further.

Whenever the word "covenant" is used, make the same sign movement given for "testament," but use the "C" hands, palms facing downward, instead of the "T's."

# TESTIFY

Bear witness; give evidence.

Touch the lips with the right "T" hand, palm facing left. Then move the right hand forward away from the lips.

# TESTIMONY

Statement of a witness under oath, used for proof; evidence.

Touch the left open hand, palm facing front right diagonal, with the right "T" hand, palm facing front left diagonal. Move both hands forward. It is the same as the sign for "show," except that the right hand is in the "T" position.

BOTH HANDS

# THEOLOGY

Doctrine concerning God and his relation to man and the universe; the study of divine things or religious truths.

With both hands in the "T" position, palms facing each other, place them at eye or forehead level in front of self. Move both hands forward and backward at least twice. It conveys the idea of a doctrine or teaching about God and his relation to man and his world.

# THORN

A sharp-pointed growth on a stem or branch of a tree or plant.

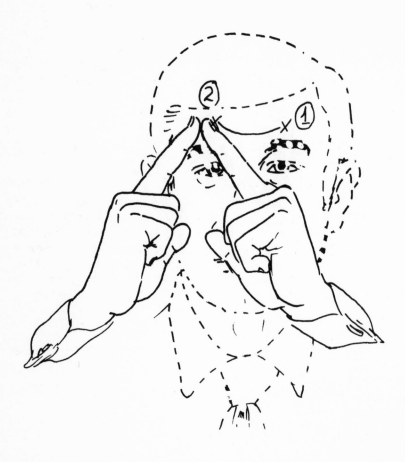

Have the right index finger touch the left index finger, both palms facing each other. Then touch the right index finger with the left index finger. Do this alternatively as you move the hands from the left to the right forehead.

# TITHE

One-tenth.

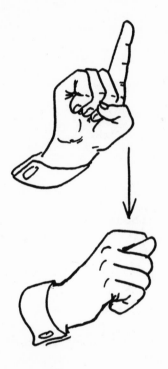

Make a sign for "one" (1). Move the hand down a little as if to write a fraction in the air. While moving the right hand down, change the sign from "one" to "T."

# TRACT

Little book or pamphlet on a religious subject.

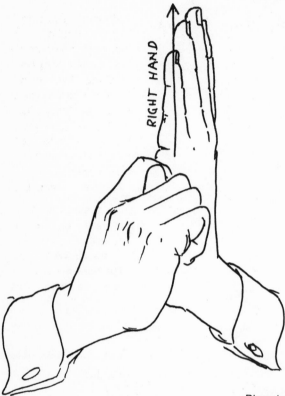

RIGHT HAND

Place in front of you the left open hand, palm facing rear right diagonal. Touch the outer edge of the little left finger with the right "T" hand, palm facing the edge of the left little finger, near the wrist. Now move the right "T" hand upward across the little finger, ending the motion near the fingertip.

## TRANSLATE

Change from one language into another; change into other words.

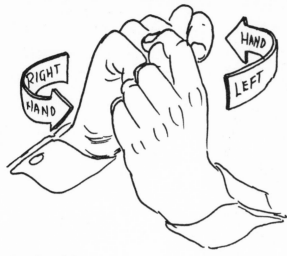

Bring to touch both "T" hands, palms facing each other and the closed fingers touching. Now turn the wrists to the right so as to bring the right to the front and the left hand to the back. It is the same as the sign for "interpret," except for the "T's."

## TRESPASS

Go beyond the limits of what is right or proper; do wrong; sin.

Position the index finger of the left hand skyward, palm facing right, in front of you. Then touch the left index finger with the right "T" hand, palm facing forward. Now veer the right hand off to the right away from the left index finger in a forward arc.

# TRIBULATION

Great trouble; severe trial.

With both hands in the "T" position, palms facing each other, place the right hand at the right forehead level and the left hand at the left side of the forehead. Move the right hand in a counterclockwise motion and the left hand in a clockwise motion. It is the same as the sign for "trouble," except for the "T" stance.

# TRINITY

Union of Father, Son and Holy Spirit in one divine nature.

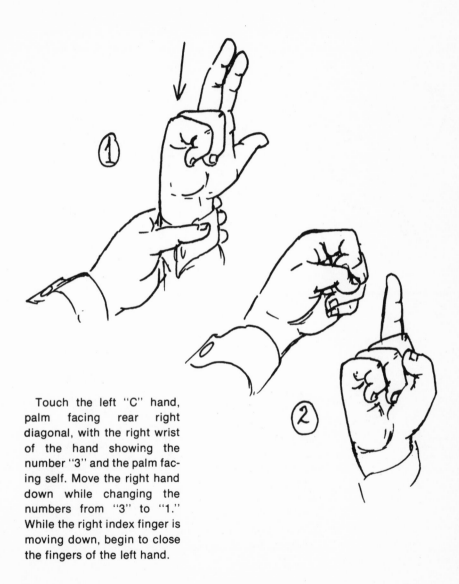

Touch the left "C" hand, palm facing rear right diagonal, with the right wrist of the hand showing the number "3" and the palm facing self. Move the right hand down while changing the numbers from "3" to "1." While the right index finger is moving down, begin to close the fingers of the left hand.

## UNITE

Join together; join in action, feeling, et cetera.

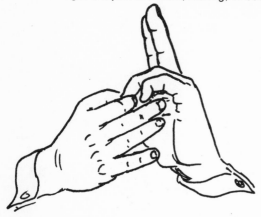

Place the left "U" hand, the palm facing the right shoulder, in front of self. Hook the thumb and index fingers of the left hand with the index finger and thumb of the right hand. The sign is the same as that for "join," except that the left hand is in the "U" stance.

## USHER

Person who shows people to their seats in a church.

Place the left open hand, palm facing forward at a slant, in front of self. Touch the left palm with the fingertips of the right "U" hand. Move both hands forward. Add the sign for "-er."

# VENGEANCE

Punishment in turn for wrong; revenge.

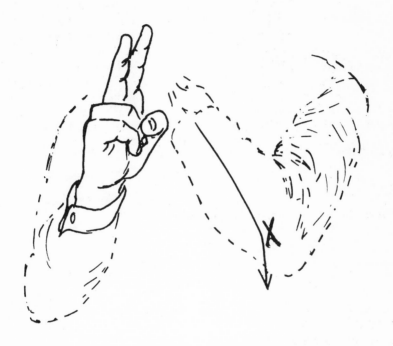

Bring the right "V" hand down so as to let the outer edge of the "V" index finger brush against the tip of the left elbow. It is the same as the sign for "punishment," except that the right hand is in the "V" position.

# VERSE

Short division of a chapter in the Bible.

Place the right "G" hand, palm facing front left diagonal, on the left open hand, palm facing front right diagonal. Move the right hand across the palm to the right or backward toward the right shoulder as if you are showing a certain section of the Scriptures on a page.

# VESPER

Evening; evening prayer, hymn or service.

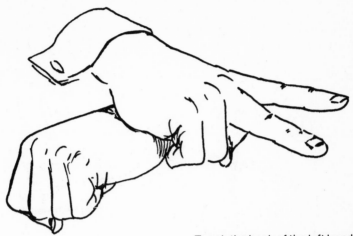

Touch the back of the left hand, palm down, with the wrist of the right "V" hand. Make the sign for "evening" in the "V" position.

# VICARIOUS

Done or suffered for others; felt by sharing in other's experience; taking the place of another.

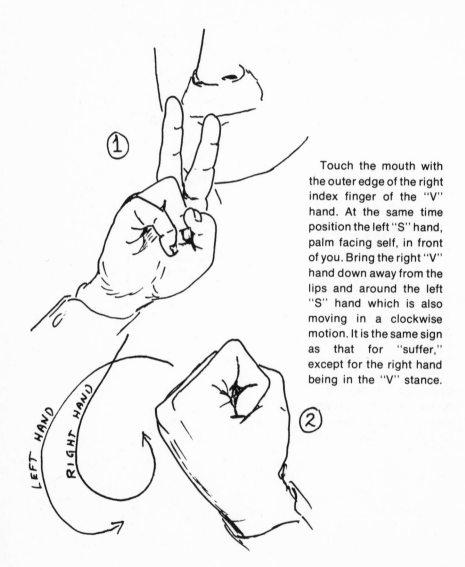

Touch the mouth with the outer edge of the right index finger of the "V" hand. At the same time position the left "S" hand, palm facing self, in front of you. Bring the right "V" hand down away from the lips and around the left "S" hand which is also moving in a clockwise motion. It is the same sign as that for "suffer," except for the right hand being in the "V" stance.

# VILE

Very bad; disgusting; poor, mean, and lowly.

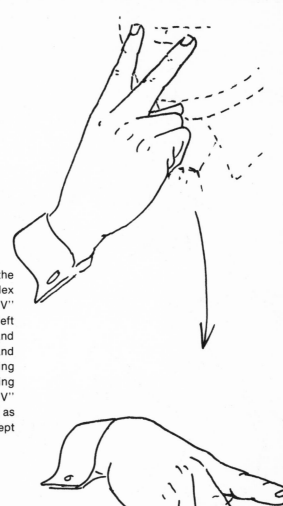

Touch the lips with the outer edge of the index finger of the right "V" hand, palm facing rear left diagonal. Move the hand away from the lips and then downward, ending with the palm facing downward in the "V" position. It is the same as the sign for "bad," except for the right "V."

# VISION

Power of seeing; something seen in a dream or imagination.

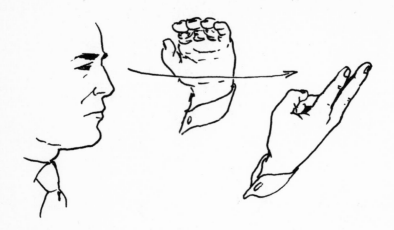

Place the right "V" hand at eye level in front of self, palm facing toward you. At the same time, position the left hand a little above and beyond the right hand, the left palm facing downward. Now move the right hand forward, the "V" fingertips brushing the left finger area.

## WICKED

Bad; evil; sinful.

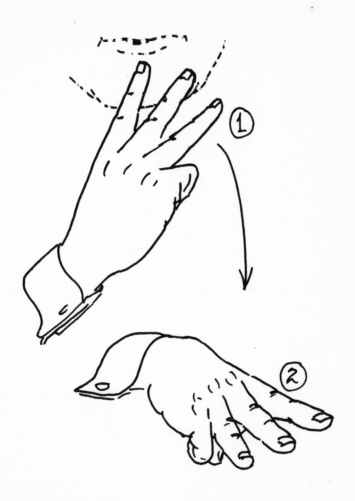

Touch the lips with the right "W" hand, the palm facing self. Move the right hand away from the lips and then down with the palm facing downward. It is the same as the sign for "bad," except for the "W."

## WITNESS

(verb) Give evidence of; sign (a document) as a witness. (noun) Person who saw something happen; person who is able to give evidence of.

BOTH HANDS FORWARD

With the left open palm facing front right diagonal and the fingers pointing upward, touch it with the right "W" hand, palm facing front left diagonal. Move both hands forward. This is the same as the sign for "show," except for the "W" position of the right hand.

# INDEX

| | Page | | Page |
|---|---|---|---|
| Adultery | 1 | Damn (ation) | 42 |
| Altar | 2 | Dare | 43 |
| Angel | 3 | Deacon | 43 |
| Anoint | 4 | Dedicate (ion) | 44 |
| Apostasy (Apostate) | 5 | Denomination | 45 |
| Apostle | 6 | Deny (ial) | 46 |
| Atone(ment) | 7 | Department | 46 |
| Attitude | 8 | Destiny | 47 |
| Authority | 9 | Devil (Satan) | 47 |
| Backslide | 10 | Devote (ion) | 48 |
| Baptist | 11 | Disciple | 49 |
| Baptize(ism) | 12 | Discipline | 50 |
| Believe (belief) | 13 | Divine | 50 |
| Beatitudes | 14 | Doctrine | 51 |
| Bible | 15 | Doom | 51 |
| Bible | 16 | Easter | 52 |
| Blasphemy | 17 | Effective | 53 |
| Bless (ing) | 18 | Elect | 54 |
| Blood | 19 | Epistle | 55 |
| Board of Deacons | 20 | Eternal | 56 |
| Burden | 21 | Ethics (al) | 56 |
| Celebrate(tion) | 22 | Evangelical (ism) | 57 |
| Chapter | 23 | Evangelist | 57 |
| Character | 24 | Everlasting | 57 |
| Choir | 25 | Exalt (ation) | 58 |
| Christ | 26 | Example (emblem) | 59 |
| Christian | 26 | Exhort (ation) | 60 |
| Church | 27 | Faith | 61 |
| Cleanse | 28 | Faithful | 62 |
| Clergy | 29 | Fast | 62 |
| Communion | 30 | Fault | 63 |
| Condemn(ation) | 31 | Favor | 63 |
| Conscience | 32 | Field | 64 |
| Consecrate(tion) | 33 | Flesh | 65 |
| Convert (sion) | 34 | Flood | 66 |
| Convict (ion) | 35 | Follow (er) | 67 |
| Corrupt (ion) | 36 | Foretell | 68 |
| Covenant | 37 | Forever | 69 |
| Creed | 38 | Forgive (ness) | 69 |
| Cross | 39 | Freewill | 70 |
| Crown | 40 | Fruit | 71 |
| Crucify (ixion) | 41 | Funeral | 72 |

| | Page | | Page |
|---|---|---|---|
| Glory (ify) | 72 | Memorial | 104 |
| God | 73 | Mercy | 105 |
| Godly | 73 | Merit | 106 |
| Gospel | 74 | Minister | 107 |
| Grace | 75 | Ministry (Missionary) | 108 |
| Grave | 76 | Miracle | 109 |
| Guilty | 76 | Mission (missionary) | 109 |
| Heaven | 77 | Moral (ity) | 110 |
| Hebrew | 78 | Mortal | 111 |
| Hell | 79 | Motive | 112 |
| Holy Spirit | 80 | Mourn | 113 |
| Hosanna | 81 | Music | 113 |
| Hymn | 81 | Mystery | 114 |
| Hypocrite | 82 | Myth | 114 |
| Idol | 82 | Nature | 115 |
| Immortal (ity) | 83 | Neighbor | 116 |
| Incarnate (ion) | 84 | Oath (Vow, Swear) | 117 |
| Infinite | 84 | Observe | 118 |
| Inspire (ation) | 85 | Occasion | 118 |
| Interpret(ation) | 86 | Offer | 119 |
| Israel | 87 | Offering | 120 |
| Jerusalem | 88 | Omnipotent | 121 |
| Jesus | 89 | Omnipresent | 121 |
| Jew (ish) | 89 | Omniscient | 122 |
| Kingdom | 90 | Opportunity | 123 |
| Lamb of God | 91 | Ordinance | 123 |
| Law | 92 | Organization | 124 |
| Layman | 92 | Own | 124 |
| Legal (ism) | 93 | Parable | 125 |
| Life | 93 | Pardon | 125 |
| Longing | 94 | Passion | 126 |
| Lord | 95 | Passover | 127 |
| Loyal (ty) | 96 | Patriarch | 128 |
| Lord's Supper | 97 | Peace | 129 |
| Magnify | 98 | Penalty | 130 |
| Majesty | 99 | Personal | 131 |
| Manifest (ation) | 99 | Personality | 132 |
| Master | 100 | Pharisee | 132 |
| Material (ism) | 100 | Plead | 133 |
| Mature (ity) | 101 | Pledge | 134 |
| Meditate (ion) | 102 | Priest | 135 |
| Mediator | 103 | Profess | 136 |

| | Page | | Page |
|---|---|---|---|
| Program | 137 | Spirit | 160 |
| Prophecy | 138 | Steward | 160 |
| Prophet | 138 | Storm (wind) | 161 |
| Psalm | 139 | Stray | 162 |
| Pure | 139 | Struggle | 163 |
| Rabbi | 140 | Submit (mission) | 163 |
| Race | 141 | Substance | 164 |
| Ransom | 142 | Subtle | 164 |
| Rebel (lion) | 143 | Superstition | 165 |
| Reconcile (ation) | 143 | Supplication | 165 |
| Redeem (er) | 144 | Supply | 166 |
| Reform (ation) | 144 | Symbol | 167 |
| Refuse (al) | 145 | Talent | 168 |
| Religion | 146 | Temple | 169 |
| Religious | 146 | Ten Commandments | 170 |
| Repent (ance) | 147 | Testament (covenant) | 171 |
| Reprove | 147 | Testify | 172 |
| Revere (nt, nce) | 148 | Testimony | 172 |
| Revival | 148 | Theology | 173 |
| Revive | 149 | Thorn | 174 |
| Righteous (ness) | 149 | Tithe | 175 |
| Sabbath | 150 | Tract | 176 |
| Sacrifice | 151 | Translate | 177 |
| Saint | 151 | Trespass | 177 |
| Sake | 152 | Tribulation | 178 |
| Sanctify (ication) | 153 | Trinity | 179 |
| Sanctuary | 153 | Unite | 180 |
| Salvation (save) | 154 | Usher | 180 |
| Satisfy (ication) | 154 | Vengeance | 181 |
| Scripture | 155 | Verse | 182 |
| Self-centered | 156 | Vesper | 183 |
| Seminary | 157 | Vicarious | 184 |
| Serve (Service) | 157 | Vile | 185 |
| Sin (ner) | 158 | Vision | 186 |
| Social | 158 | Wicked | 187 |
| Society | 159 | Witness | 188 |